ED ROSENTHAL'S
MARIJUANA
GROWING TIPS

D1738279

QUICK AMERICAN PUBLISHING

P.O. BOX 429477
SAN FRANCISCO, CA
94142–9477

Ed Rosenthal's Marijuana Growing Tips
ISBN: 0–932551–05–X
copyright © 1986 by Ed Rosenthal

Published by **Quick American Publishing**
P.O.Box 429477 San Francisco, CA 94142–9477

First Printing : October 1986
Current Printing : 9 8 7 6

The material herein is intended for information and reference only.
The author and publisher advise against any application of the
procedures herein if they involve breaking the law or any hazard to
persons and/or property. The reader is cautioned about the use of
drugs, and advised to consult a personal physician. However,
we urge readers to support. N.O.R.M.L. in its efforts to secure
passage of fair marijuana legislation.

Acknowledgements

Project Editor : Sebastian Orfali
Developmental Editor : Jim Schreiber
Data Entry : Judith Abrahms
Manuscript Editor : Judith Abrahms
Coding for Typesetting : Nancy Krompotich
Typesetting : Nickel Ads
Photograph Conversion : John Shea
Cover Design : Brian Groppe
Layout & Production : Brian Groppe
Printing : Delta Lithograph

Contents

Preface

Ed Rosenthal has documented the transformation of pot cultivation in the USA more successfully than any other writer. His various books, including *The Indoor/Outdoor Highest Quality Growers Guide, Deluxe Edition Marijuana Growers Guide, Marijuana Beer* and *Marijuana Growers Handbook: Indoor/Greenhouse Edition* have all together sold more than a million of copies. His collumns in *High Times Magazine* have earned him the sobriquet "The Ann Landers of Marijuana". He has been a tireless advocate and organizer, unafraid to put himself on the line for change in marijuana laws. Recently, he has taken up helping defendants in marijuana cases as an expert witness.

Readers acquainted with Ed's writing will welcome this book for its breadth of topics, not discussed elsewhere. New readers will find it a good introduction to his writing. His down home, humorous style is appealing to to the average pothead as well as the government officials responsible for enforcing the country's drug laws. People on both sides of the issue welcome his work.

Flowering sativa. It is light and fluffy with long, elegant hairs.

Chapter One
Choosing a Cannabis Variety

Seed catalogs are fascinating. For instance, the tomato section of a typical catalog devotes pages and pages to the different tomato varieties. Some are early bloomers, others mold-or-wilt-resistant; they produce fruits from the size of a cherry to that of a grapefruit; some are good for canning, others for juice. There are even square tomatoes. Each variety was developed by researchers to meet a specific need.

When cannabis becomes legal, commercial seed houses will develop varieties to suit each gardener's requirements: "Let's see, I'd like something that grows about six feet in six weeks, develops a giant cola, matures in sixty days, smells like cheap perfume, tastes like heady champagne, and takes me to the moon."

There are already illicit seed co-ops functioning on a small scale. Last season, in certain western states, breeders commanded five dollars per seed for acclimated varieties. Even at that price, growers consider these seeds worth buying: they view the seed money as a minor investment in view of the total value of the harvest. Rooted cuttings from proven outstanding plants can sell for $15 per plant or more.

When it comes to choosing a variety, commercial growers are concerned with several factors, among them: branching habits, drought resistance, ease of manicuring, color, and uniform ripening. Of primary importance is the ripening time. Most outdoor growers want plants that mature early, before the arrival of frost, thieves, and law enforcement. Indoors, commercial growers want compact plants that ripen quickly and uniformly, so that light and space are used most efficiently.

Commercial growers are also interested in the plant's yield. Some plants bud heavily and grow thick colas; others do not. A heavy-yielding plant may be worth twice as much as a lighter-yielding one. The type of high does not seem to be an important marketing factor, though the yield, the aroma, the taste, and the bud appearance are important in determining the price.

Home growers, however, have different priorities. The yield or growth time may not be as important as the type of high. Home gardens often contain several varieties of marijuana, some taking as long as six months to mature.

Seeds-people have concentrated their efforts on developing indica hybrids, which are desirable because of their early maturing (September to early October), and because of the heavy yields available from these compact plants. Some indica varieties are cold- or drought-resistant. Although the indicas exhibit a range of highs, I find most to be heavy and stupefying.

Commercial growers have tended to overlook potency and quality of high in their search for plants that mature early. Their reasoning is that they would rather have a poorer-quality sinsemilla harvest than no harvest at all. Very much like the square tomatoes I mentioned earlier, commercial varieties of cannabis ship well but are tasteless.

Turning to the sativa varieties, most mature too late (three to four months later than the indicas) for outdoor cultivation, and hence are avoided by most commercial growers. Sativas also tend to grow tall with loose branching, so that their yield per square foot is less than that of indicas. However, the quality of high from sativa

Wiscany marijuana, displayed on a map of the region near Madison, Wisconsin, where it was grown. This variety is the result of several generations of careful breeding. It is ready to harvest before October 1st.

grown in the equatorial regions (Colombia, Congo, Nigeria, Kenya and Laos) is unsurpassed. It is unfortunate that only the home grower (and his/her friends) can experience these highs; they're just not available commercially.

Sativa varieties grow all over the world. At the 15th parallel, in Jamaica and Mexico, there are some excellent sativa varieties that mature earlier than their equatorial cousins. Thailand is also at the 15th parallel, but its plants have a long growing season. Most of the commercial varieties available at the 30th parallel are indicas such as Kush, Afghani, and Lebanese. But in the Southern Hemisphere at the 30th parallel, Southern African varieties will mature early and are often quite potent.

Durban poison, Capetown gold, Lesotho brown, and Zuluweed are vigorous, short-to medium-height plants with internodes of up to eight inches. They are also the earliest-flowering and fastest-maturing plants ever introduced in the United States.

Like most cannabis varieties found at the 30th parallel, South African plants tend to vary within a specific population. This is an evolutionary technique of survival for species situated in an environment with a varying climate.

Moroccan plants are grown close together so that they have one main flowering stem. It ripens early, but is not very intoxicating.

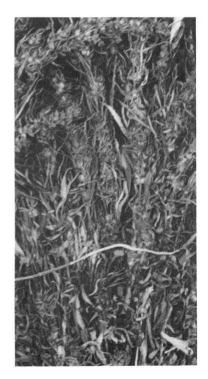

African varieties are not usually imported into the United States, but find their market in Europe; there is usually a large number of Africans available in Amsterdam, for example.

Sativa varieties grown above the 30th parallel have been used for hemp, and are commonly regarded as having no psychoactive qualities. But reports from the Midwest, where this "hemp" has escaped from cultivation and grows in wild stands, indicate that potency varies from terrible headache-weed to pot that delivers a fair buzz. Cultivators in areas where such varieties of sativa are growing may wish to use these in their breeding programs because such plants are well acclimated to the area, having survived with no human help. With a little patience, high potency and aroma can be bred into this hardy stock, which matures every year.

By controlling all pollination and keeping detailed records, it's easy to develop a simple breeding program, and within five or six generations you can develop and stabilize several characteristics.

Commercial breeders grow large numbers of plants from which a few outstanding specimens are chosen. Their descendants are again selected, and are often crossed with varieties that have other desirable traits. For instance, a hemp plant that matures very early might be crossed with a potent, later-maturing plant. The first generation will be fairly uniform. The second generation will sort out into early and late plants of varying potency. If only early/potent plants are selected for further breeding, this pair of characteristics will stabilize after several generations. Usually, commercial seeds-people try to stabilize many characteristics at once so that the plants will be uniform.

A sophisticated breeding program can be developed indoors under controlled conditions. Many environmental factors can be easily controlled and the plants bred throughout the year. By setting the light cycle at 15 hours per day (the number of hours of daylight available in late July), the researcher can select early-maturing plants. Later-maturing plants may need longer periods of uninterrupted darkness, approximating late autumn or winter, before they flower profusely.

Indoors, full-sized plants can be grown in one-to two-gallon containers. About two square feet of space per plant are required. Plants can be selected after a few weeks of growth, so that less space is required and the breeding program can be speeded up to between three and five generations per year. Taking cuttings is the only way of preserving the exact genetic makeup of any plant. You may wish to keep an outstanding plant for garden clones or for breeding.

Over the years, American cultivators have developed tens of thousands of varieties. American sinsemilla is now the most potent in the world. Traditionally, marijuana cultivation extended only to the 30th parallel. However, American growers have expanded the growing area to Maine and Alaska.

Novice cultivators would do well to borrow seed from a successful local grower whose pot they especially like. That way, they know that the plants will mature in time and will be pleasant to smoke.

Typical afghani flowering top.

Chapter Two
Selecting Seeds

Choosing the right seed is probably the most important decision a grower makes.

The seed (actually the fruit of the cannabis plant), properly known as an achene, contains the germ plasm or genetic material. This genetic material determines the plant's potential size, shape, time to maturity, and cannabinoid content. Given adequate amounts of warmth, light, water, nutrients, oxygen and carbon dioxide, the plant can achieve the full potential that is present within the seed.

By choosing seeds from plants suited to the growing conditions in your garden, you can assure yourself of a large, potent yield.

There are several factors to consider when deciding what varieties to plant: the desired high, the maturation time, and the shape of the plant.

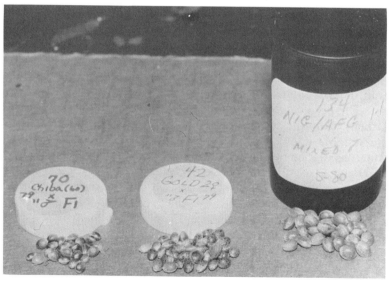

Seeds vary in size and coloring according to variety. A large seed does not necessarily mean a more potent plant.

The high is the most important factor. Choose seeds from grass that you like. Potency should not be the sole determinant — the quality of the high is just as important. The ratios and absolute amounts of the known cannabinoids that are found in any particular sample is partly genetic, much the same as with grapes. (Each variety of grape has a distinctive taste, but there are variations from year to year because of differing climatic conditions.)

Maturation time is another important characteristic, especially for outdoor growers. Most imported marijuana now comes from Colombia or other equatorial countries with a growing season of eight to ten months. Plants from these areas have a long time in which to flower and produce seeds. When equatorial plants are grown in an area with a shorter growing season, they do not have enough time to produce mature colas, or seeds, before the end of the growing season (or before the start of the hunting season).

Ragweed, or Midwestern cannabis, is descended from plants escaped from hemp fields. It was cultivated for fiber and seed from colonial times until the 1940s. Hemp matures in three to five months, depending on the variety. Unfortunately, most varieties contain large amounts of CBD, which doesn't get you high, and small amounts of THC, which does.

There are several methods you can use to get plants that will mature within the American growing season. The easiest way is to choose seeds from plants acclimated to regions situated at some distance from the equator. Marijuana from northern Mexican states, such as Sonora, Sinaloa, and Jalisco, may mature up to six weeks earlier than Colombian. Other countries that grow marijuana and have shorter growing seasons are Nepal, Afghanistan, Iran, Pakistan, and northern India.

The problem with plants from these countries is that, as the distance from the equator increases, the ratio of CBD to THC increases. Marijuana from Afghanistan, Lebanon, and Nepal — countries that lie on the 30th parallel -may have equal amounts of CBD and THC. But this is not always the case. Remember that a particular population of plants (a patch or field) evolves in response to the conditions it experiences — the microclimate — rather than to the average conditions found in the region.

Another method for producing faster-maturing strains is to develop your own strain by selecting for particular qualities. For instance, you could plant a garden using an equatorial marijuana variety. By selecting for early-flowering potent plants, you can develop your strain into a fast-maturing one after several generations.

Sativa leaf is slender with long fingers.

Sativa plant is tall and lanky with fluffy buds.

Indica leaf is wide, with short fingers.

Indica plants are squat and dense with heavy, compact buds.

Marijuana and hemp can be crossed to produce hybrids. These plants will mature earlier than the equatorial parent and will be quite hardy, but the marijuana will not be as potent or have the same quality high as the exotic parent. Another drawback is that the progeny of the F_1, or first generation — the F_2 generation — will not breed true because of differences in genetic makeup.

This means that for a uniformly flowering garden, only F_1 hybrids can be used. But growers can produce more than enough seed from just a pair of plants.

Indica (forefront) and sativa (background) were started at the same time. Notice how much taller and wider the sativa is.

To assure seed maturation, growing should be done in a greenhouse or indoors. Indoor growers can choose seeds and develop breeding programs based on the following considerations:

1. Fast development under limited-light/long-day conditions. This is similar to the light cycle experienced by northern latitude hemp plants.

2. Insect and disease resistance: some plants may not get infected when the others do. The resistance could be genetic.

3. Full bud development.

4. Ability to regenerate for multiple flowering. Indoor plants can often be regenerated after flowering by changing the light cycle.

A final consideration is the size and shape of the plant. For each garden, there is a plant of ideal size and shape. In forest areas, growers may require a tall-growing plant such as a South Korean, a northern Mexican, or a marijuana-hemp F_1 hybrid. In areas where a bushy plant might be obvious, the more diminutive Indica varieties will fit right in. Colombian plants grow into a conical shape, but can be pruned to a low bush, or trained by bending the main branch.

Home gardeners usually like to grow several varieties, so that they can see what does best in the garden. Each variety has its own look, fragrance, taste, and bouquet of cannabinoids.

Chapter Three
Cuttings

The traditional way to start a new marijuana crop is to plant seeds. About half the resulting plants will be male. The remaining females, even if their background is certain, will be of varying quality.

Most flower and vegetable seed sold in the United States is standardized. Seed of a particular variety will have uniform growth habits, harvest time, and yield. But marijuana has been bred for uniformity by only a few dedicated growers. Of course, their seed is not commercially available. Without an intensive breeding program, clones (cuttings or slips) are the only way to get a uniform crop. For an all-female crop, of known quality, growers can use either clones or plant regeneration.

Regeneration, or recropping, is a method of obtaining a second harvest from the same plant. A plant can be returned to its vegetative growth stage by letting a number of healthy shoots and leaves remain on it at the time when most of the buds are harvested. (Bring the lights back up to 18 or more hours per day and fertilize with a high-nitrogen fertilizer.) Plants growing outdoors in containers can be brought inside for another harvest using this method. In a greenhouse, the fall and winter natural light should be supplemented and extended. Within a few months the garden should be ready to be turned back into the flowering phase, which is achieved by increasing the number of hours of uninterrupted darkness (turning the light cycle down to 12 or 13 hours of light per day).

Such regeneration has several advantages. Your garden can be designed and used most efficiently because you know the plant's growth habits. Each plant's qualities are already known, so you can devise a rational breeding program.

A clone is a genetic duplicate of its parent. Clones should be made whenever you have a unique plant whose particular genetic code is worth preserving. Examples might be extremely potent, fast-growing, or early-flowering plants. A garden of these plants, given the same environmental conditions as their parents, will behave identically. They will be the same height, will have the same growth habits, will flower and ripen at the same time, and will have the same potency.

Equipment used for cutting includes: a) boiled water to float cutting b) bleach to sterilize the blade and the cutting, and used in a 5% solution (2 oz per quart) with the water to prevent infection c) rooting compound and fungicide (Rootone®) d) high phosphorous fertilizer used diluted at one-quarter recommended concentration, and e) cutting immersed in sterile water, awaiting preparation.

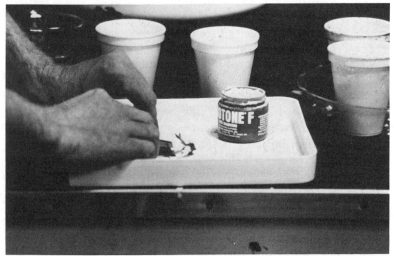

Cutting is made with a sterile blade. At least two leaf nodes (joints) are required.

As many as six clones may be made from this cutting.

Growers often make clones from all their plants while the plants are still in the vegetative growth stage. Later, after harvest and testing, they decide which clones to keep. These plants are grown under lights for their cuttings so that the grower can have a uniform crop the next spring or fall. It is essential for anyone who is performing controlled environmental experiments to use plants of a uniform genotype. Otherwise the experimenter has no way to know what's being measured.

Homogeneous or "clone" gardens have several disadvantages. Plants with identical genetic structures have similar resistance and susceptibilities to insect attack and microbial infections, and any type of degeneration is likely to spread more quickly than if the plants were of different varieties, or had simply been grown from different seeds.

As I mentioned earlier, clones from the same parent will all taste about the same and create the same high. This is fine for a commercial operation, where standardization may increase profits, but most smokers enjoy using several varieties of pot. For this reason, you may wish to culture clones of several varieties that will flower in succession.

Klone Kit®shown here is no longer available, but can be easily approximated — using 100 ml container, Styrofoam packing disks, and 15 ml of vermiculite. The clone is inserted in a hole punched in the Styrofoam, and floated in mixture of vermiculite and sterile water. The excellent hormone solution used in the Klone Kit is available from W R Research (Novato, California).

There are several cloning techniques, including air and soil layering, and tissue culture, that are used commercially to mass-produce some nursery stock. But the easiest and most familiar method of cloning is taking slips or cuttings. Cuttings can be taken at any time in a plant's life cycle, but those taken before the plant is flowering will root more easily. Larger branches sometimes exhibit white protuberances near the base of the stem. These are called adventitious roots. They appear under humid conditions, and grow readily into roots when placed in water or in various mediums. Cuttings from the lower branches, which contain less nitrogen and have a higher ratio of sugars, root somewhat faster than slips from the top of the plant, so it's wisest to take your cuttings from the bottom branches.

To take a cutting, make a clean cut with a razor, knife, or clippers. Place the cut end in water. Remove the large fan leaves so that the cuttings' water uptake capabilities won't be overtaxed. The cutting can be propagated in water, pasteurized prepackaged soil, or vermiculite-perlite mixtures. Before being placed in the medium, cuttings should be treated with a fungicidal-B[1] mix that promotes root growth, such as Rootone F.

These flourishing clones are ready for transplanting.

Place your cuttings in four-to six-inch individual pots with the stems between two and four inches deep — quart and half-gallon milk containers will work fine — and be sure to keep them in an area that gets only a moderate amount of light or they will wilt. After five days they should be fertilized with vermiculite-perlite mixture, diluted to one-quarter normal strength, once a week. Covering the cuttings with clear plastic will increase the humidity and the success rate.

Plant rooting is inhibited by lack of oxygen. To prevent this from occurring, aerate the water before use by shaking it vigorously. Cuttings that are propagated in water will do best if the water is either changed regularly, or aerated using an aquarium pump and air stone. Make sure the bubbles rise away from the stems and do not create too much turbulence, which may inhibit root growth.

Cuttings root in three to five weeks, after which time you should transplant them to larger pots. If they are growing under artificial light, introduce them to sunlight gradually so that the leaves do not burn when placed in full sunlight.

Cuttings are usually taken before flowering. However, this cutting was taken during flowering and has regenerated.

Chapter Four
Do It Hydroponically

If you've ever grown a backyard tomato, or kept a coleus alive through the winter, you have all the expertise you need to grow plants hydroponically. Quite simply, hydroponics is the method of cultivating plants without using soil. The plants are grown in a non-nutritive medium such as gravel or sand, or in lightweight, man-made materials such as perlite, vermiculite (a mineral-mica nutrient base), or Styrofoam. Nutrients are then supplied to the plants in one of two ways: either by soluble fertilizers that are dissolved in water, or by time-release fertilizers that are mixed into the medium.

The advantages of a hydroponics system over conventional horticultural methods are numerous and varied. Dry spots and root drowning do not occur. Nutrient and pH problems are largely eliminated, since the grower maintains a tight control over their concentration. There is little chance of "lockup," which occurs when nutrients are fixed in the soil and unavailable to the plant. Plants can be grown more conveniently in smaller containers. And, because there is no messing about with soil, the whole operation is easier, cleaner, and much less bothersome than it would be with conventional growing techniques.

Most hydroponic systems fall into one of two broad categories: passive and active. Passive systems, such as reservoir or wick setups, depend on the molecular action inherent in the wick or in the medium to make water available to the plant. Active systems, which include the flood, recirculating drip, and aerated water systems, use a pump to send nourishment to the plant.

Most commercially made "hobby" hydroponic systems designed for general use are built shallow and wide, so that an intensive garden with a variety of plants can be grown. However, most marijuana growers prefer to grow each plant in an individual container. Indoors, a three-gallon container is adequate. Outdoors, a five-gallon (or larger) container should be used if the water cannot be replenished frequently. Automatic systems irrigated on a regular schedule can use smaller containers, but all containers should be deep, rather than shallow, so that the roots can firmly anchor the plant.

PASSIVE HYDROPONIC SYSTEMS

The wick system is inexpensive and easy to set up and maintain. The principle underlying this type of passive system is that a length of ⅜-to ⅝-inch-thick braided nylon rope, used as a wick, will draw enough nourishment from a reservoir filled with a water/nutrient solution to keep a growing medium moist. The container, which holds a rooting medium, has wicks running along the bottom and dropping through small, tight-fitting holes to the reservoir. Keeping the holes small makes it difficult for roots to penetrate to the reservoir. By increasing the number or length of the wicks, or their thickness, you can increase the amount of water delivered to the medium. A three-gallon container should have two wicks; a five-gallon container, three wicks. The wick system is self-regulating: the amount of water delivered depends on the amount lost through evaporation or transpiration.

Each medium has a maximum saturation level. Beyond that point, an increase in the number of wicks will not increase the level of moisture. A 1-1-1 combination of vermiculite, perlite, and Styrofoam makes a convenient medium, because the components are lightweight and readily available. Vermiculite alone sometimes develops too air-free an environment and becomes compacted, so that a tall plant might tip over. Perlite, which doesn't compress, keeps the medium loose and airy. Styrofoam beads hold no water, and therefore help keep the medium drier. Pea-sized chopped polyurethane foam, gravel, sand, and lava can also be used to make a medium. In any case, the bottom inch of the container should be filled only with vermiculite, which is very absorbent, so that the wicks have a good medium for moisture transfer.

A wick system can be constructed as follows: Cut four holes, about ½"in diameter, in the bottom of a three-gallon container. Run the wicks through the holes so that each end extends about three inches outside the container. Unbraid the wicks to aid absorption. Put two bricks in the bottom of a deep tray (an oil drip pan will do fine), into which you've poured the water/nutrient solution, then place the container on the bricks so that the wicks are immersed in the solution. Keep replacing the solution as it is absorbed.

A variation on this system can be constructed by using an additional outer container rather than a tray. With this method, less water is lost through evaporation. To make sure that the containers fit together and come apart easily, place the bricks in the bottom of

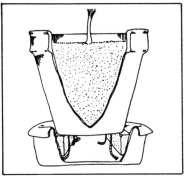

The wick system. A plastic container with 4½ "nylon wicks. The container is sitting on two bricks in a plastic oil pan.

The reservoir system. A plastic container sitting in an oil pan which is kept filled with water. The bottom half of this container is filled with lava and the top half with vermiculite.

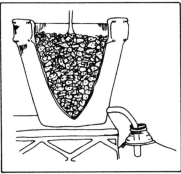

The flood system. A simple flood system in drained position.

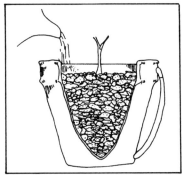

The flood system, con't Container being flooded manually. This unit could easily be used as a component in a larger, automatic system by attaching the tube to a pipe leading to a central reservoir and pump.

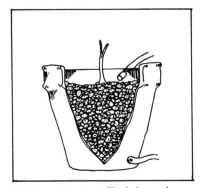

The drip emitter system. The drainage tube can lead back to a central reservoir or the water can be recirculated using a small aquarium pump.

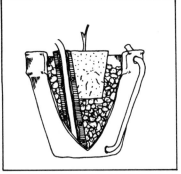

The aerated water system. A plastic column allows air to flow freely upward. The water circulates and picks up oxygen from the air at the surface and from the bubbles.

the outer container. Fill the outer container with the water/nutrient solution until it comes to just below the bottom of the inner container.

The reservoir system is even simpler than the wick system. For this setup you need only fill the bottom two or three inches of a 12-inch-deep container with a coarse, porous, inert medium such as lava, ceramic beads, or chopped pottery, and then pour in the nutrient/water solution. Variations on this method include a plastic flower pot or plastic growing bag sitting directly in a tray or pail of the nutrient/water solution.

All passive systems should be watered from the top down, so that any surface buildup of nutrients caused by evaporation will be washed back to the bottom.

The drip method, using a vermiculite, perlite, sand mix with nutrient solution in the water is easily set up with materials available at garden supply stores.

This individual reservoir is easy to set up and maintain. Lava is used as the medium in the 3½ gallon container placed on a 3 inch tray. Nutrient solution is added to the top of the tray. When the tray is empty it is refilled with plain water. Additional nutrients are added about once a month.

ACTIVE HYDROPONIC SYSTEMS

The flood system consists of a tub or container holding a medium that is completely flooded on a regular basis, usually once, twice, or three times daily, depending on the growth stage and environmental factors. The medium holds enough moisture between irrigations to meet the needs of the plant. First-generation commercial greenhouses using this method were usually built with long beds of gravel that were systematically flooded. Today, the flood system is most often used with individual containers, with each container attached to the reservoir by tubing or by a leak-proof seal.

For watering convenience, a kiddie-pool was used as a reservoir for this indoor garden.

With this system, growers have a choice of mediums, including sand, pebbles, chopped-up rubber tires, pea-sized lava, gravel, and vermiculite-perlite-Styrofoam mixtures. A recommended mixture for this setup would be one part each of perlite and Styrofoam and two parts vermiculite, or one part vermiculite and four parts lava. (Note: Because perlite and Styrofoam are lighter than water and will float if this system is fully flooded, neither should be used alone as a medium in this type of system.)

A simple flood system can be constructed using a container with a tube attached to its bottom and a one-gallon jug. Fill the container with the medium. Each day pour the water/nutrient solution from the jug into the container, holding the tube up high enough that no water drains out. Then let tube down so that the water drains back into the jug. Some water will have been absorbed by the medium, so fill the jug to its original level before the next

Plastic bags are convenient containers, but care should be taken not to disturb the roots when moving them.

watering. The plants' water needs increase during the lighted part of the daily cycle, so the best time to water is when the light cycle begins. If the medium does not hold enough between waterings, water more frequently. Flood systems can be automated by using an air pump to push water from the reservoir into the growing unit.

Drip emitters are complete systems that can be bought in nurseries or garden shops. They have been used for years to water individual plants in gardens and homes. They can also be used with a central reservoir and a pump so that the water/nutrient solution will be redistributed periodically. If you choose this system, make sure you buy self-cleaning emitters so that the dissolved nutrients do not clog with salt deposits. Start pumping about a gallon every six hours during the daylight hours. Drip emitters can be used with semiporous mediums such as ceramic beads, lava, gravel, sand, or perlite-vermiculite-Styrofoam mixtures.

The aerated water system is probably the most complex of the hydroponic systems, and because it allows the least margin for error, it should be used only by growers with previous hydroponic experience. To put together an aerated water system, you must first construct a clear air channel in your container. This is done by inserting a plastic tube cut with holes through the medium. Then a fish tank aerator is placed at the bottom of the plastic tube. The air channel allows the air to circulate without disturbing the roots, and the roots use the oxygen dissolved in the water.

Germination

In most systems, with most mediums, seeds can be germinated in the unit, but mediums made of large pieces, such as lava or pea gravel, will not hold seeds in place. Make little beds of vermiculite in a coarser medium and plant the seeds in these beds.

Aerated water units cannot be used to germinate seeds. Instead, start them in peat pellets or in small pots filled with vermiculite or vermiculite-based mix. Transplant them when they are two weeks old. Cuttings and rooted cuttings can also be planted in hydroponic units.

Nutrients

Choose a fertilizer designed for hydroponic growing. Make sure that it supplies adequate amounts of nitrogen during early growth stages. Typical hydroponic fertilizers have nutrient ratios of 9-5-10 or 18-6-16 (nitrogen-phosphorus-potassium, or N-P-K). Fertilizers used for later growth should have lower ratios of N. In addition to N-P-K, the fertilizer should supply secondary and micro-nutrients, which will be listed on the label of the fertilizer package. Some fertilizers seem to be deficient in magnesium (correct this by using Epsom salts) and iron-zinc-manganese (available in combination at large nurseries).

The pH level can also affect solubility of nutrients, so try to keep the pH of the water between 6.3 and 6.8. (The easiest way to gauge your pH level is by using pH paper. You can pick some up at any garden shop.) Before mixing the nutrients into the water, adjust the pH using sulfuric, nitric, or citric acid if it is too high; lime or baking soda if it is too low.

Whatever system you decide to use, once the nutrient/water solution has been added, replacement water should be nutrient-free. If you notice a slowing of growth, or a nutrient deficiency, adjust the nutrient solution. For instance, if the plants show signs of a potassium deficiency (necrotic leaf tips and edges, yellowing of leaves), add potassium. Once the nutrient problem has been corrected, the plant will respond quickly and the improvement should be apparent within a few days.

About every month or two, replace the water/nutrient solution. The discarded water makes a good garden fertilizer. Every other time you change the water, rinse the medium with clear water to wash away any salts that have been left before adding new nutrient/water solution.

How to Make a Universal Hydroponic Unit

It is easy to make a unit that can be used for all the systems described in this chapter. Take a two-to five-gallon plastic container and cut a hole near the bottom large enough to snugly hold a plastic tube with a minimum inside diameter of ⅜". Cut the tube three inches taller than the pot. Push 1½" of the tube through the hole from the outside and affix the end to the inside bottom using a silicone or other type of glue, or PVC tape. Caulk the seal with plastic glue or caulk.

Making a tight, leak-proof seal can be difficult if the plastics are incompatible. Roughing out both surfaces sometimes helps. Another way of attaching the tube is to use a piece of threaded plastic pipe, two washers and two nuts. Tighten the two nuts on either side of the container wall.

It is advisable to use clear plastic tubing so that you can see the water level and drainage action. If you're using a two-container system, such as the wick or reservoir system, it is still easier to use an outer container with a tube, which facilitates draining. (Some commercial units have no drainage, which makes it difficult to change the nutrient/water solution.)

Chapter Five
Good News for Late Planters

Marijuana can be successfully started in late July and still come in early in the fall. This makes it easy for people who have not had a chance to do their planting early, and allows growers to increase the size of their crops. Late plants will not be as big or yield as much as earlier plants, but their quality will be just as high.

Starting plants indoors is probably the easiest way to begin. The plant's initial growth can be spurred by using metal halides and a CO_2-enriched atmosphere. Under good conditions, and depending on the variety planted, the plants should be six inches to one foot high within two weeks, and should grow at a rate of six inches to one foot per week for the next six weeks. A six-week-old plant will be four to six feet tall; a four-week-old plant, two to three feet; a three-week-old plant, one to two feet. Of course, the plants will not fill out as an outdoor plant would. As long as they get enough water, they won't be damaged by the hot August sun.

There is one problem with starting plants indoors. Unless the natural light cycle is modified, they will start to flower almost immediately if they are early-maturing varieties. To modify the light cycle, the night must be interrupted, because the plants determine their flowering time according to the number of hours of uninterrupted darkness. Shining a light over the entire surface of the plant in the middle of the darkness cycle will stop the plant from going into its flowering stage. A powerful flashlight, fluorescent light, or incandescent light will do. Car headlights also work well. The darkness cycle should be interrupted every night, until you wish the plants to go into the flowering stage.

Unless the plants are to be brought indoors for finishing, or there is a long growing season, light modification should be terminated by August 15. The plants will start to flower almost immediately and will mature near their normal time.

Backyard growers may find it convenient to grow plants in portable containers so they can move the plants between the basement or garage and the outdoors. Then they can manipulate the light cycle to their needs, using an artificial source such as metal halides or fluorescents to supplement the natural light. Should there

Blackout room. Note opaque plastic used to shield plants from light.

be an overcast or rainy day, the plants will still get plenty of bright light indoors. At night the plants can be locked up safe and sound, away from the greedy hands of thieves. Also, spotting helicopters will be unable to locate the plants while they are sheltered.

To increase outdoor plant growth during the early stages, spray the plants with carbonated water several times a day. Make sure not to use club soda, which contains salt. Instead, make your own with a home soda maker, which uses CO_2 cartridges, or buy seltzer, which has no salt added.

You can also make carbonated water using a CO_2 tank and attached hose emptying into a container of water. If the container can be safely pressurized, the amount of CO_2 dissolved in the water will increase. Dry ice, which is frozen CO_2, can also be used.

If the young plants are sprayed several times a day, their growth can be speeded up considerably. As the plants grow, it becomes less cost-effective to spray them, but it is still worthwhile.

The opaque cover is removed to expose plants to light. This way, the photoperiod of the light cycle can be controlled.

Smaller plants may be started months later than their larger sisters, and will flower at about the same time. Their potency will be about the same, since it is based not on their chronological age, but on their maturity. Although yields on small plants are low, these plants can be placed much closer together. (In Morocco, in many cases, plants are grown by broadcast seeding, which may produce as many as 25 plants per square foot.) A 10′ x 10′ area, a total of 100 square feet, covered with plants one to two feet high in four-inch pots, placed nine per square foot, would yield a good stash. Each plant would consist primarily of a main stem with a joint's worth of buds on it — roughly 900 joints.

Chapter Six
It's a Gas

Plant growth is determined by five factors: heat, water, nutrients, light, and carbon dioxide. An insufficient amount of any one of these can seriously debilitate your crop.

In an indoor environment, heat, water, and nutrients never pose any problem to the cultivator: ample supplies of each are readily available. Light is provided by using natural light and/or a variety of artificial sources (see Chapter 10). This leaves carbon dioxide (CO_2).

CO_2 is a gas that makes up about .03 percent (300 parts per million, or "ppm") of the atmosphere. It is not dangerous. It is one of the basic raw materials (water is the other) used by plants in the act of photosynthesis. And it can make those little buggers grow like crazy.

When plants are growing in an enclosed area, there is a limited amount of CO_2 for them to use. When this CO_2 is used up, the plant's photosynthesis stops. Only as more CO_2 is provided can it use light to continue the process. Adequate amounts of CO_2 may be easily replaced in well-ventilated areas. However, a more-than-adequate amount — .2 percent (2000 ppm), or six times the amount usually found in the atmosphere — can increase the growth rate by up to a factor of five. For this reason, many commercial nurseries provide CO_2-enriched air for their plants.

The two most economical and convenient ways to give your plants all the CO_2 they'll ever need are: (1) use a CO_2 generator that burns natural gas or kerosene, and (2) use a CO_2 tank with a regulator.

First, of course, you must find out how much CO_2 is needed to bring the growing area up to the ideal level of 2000 ppm. To do this, multiply the volume of the growing area (length × height × width) by .002. The result represents the number of cubic feet of gas required to reach optimum CO_2 range. For instance, a room that measure 13′ × 18′ × 12′ contains 2,808 cubic feet; 2,808 × .002 equals 5.6 cubic feet.

The easiest way to supply the gas is to use a CO_2 tank. All the equipment you'll need can be obtained from a welding supply store. The tank, which comes in 20-and 50-pound sizes, can be bought or rented. (A 50-gallon tank, filled, has a gross weight of 170 pounds.) To regulate dispersal of the gas, a "combination flow meter regulator" is required. It regulates the flow to between 10 and 50 cubic feet per hour. A solenoid valve turns the flow meter on and off. This can be operated manually, or by a 24-hour timer. The timer should be a multicycle one, so that the valve can be turned on and off several times each day. If the growing room is small, a short-range timer is needed. Most timers are calibrated in ½-hour increments, but a short-range timer can keep the valve open for just a few minutes if necessary.

To find out how long the valve should remain open, divide the number of cubic feet of gas required (in our example, 5.6 cubic feet) by the flow rate. For instance, if the flow rate is 10 cubic feet per hour, 5.6 divided by 10 equals .56 hours, or 33.6 minutes (.56 × 60 minutes   33.6). At 30 cubic feet per hour, on the other hand, the number of minutes would be 5.6 divided by 30, then multiplied by 60, or 11.2 minutes.

Be sure to place the tank in an area where it can be replaced easily. Run a hose from the top of the tank unit to the top of the garden. CO_2 is cooler and heavier than air and will flow downward, reaching the tops of the plants first.

Gas and kerosene generators work by burning hydrocarbons that release heat and create carbon dioxide and water. Each pound of fuel burned produces about 3 pounds of CO_2, 1½ pounds of water, and about 21,800 BTUs (British Thermal Units) of heat.

Nursery supply houses sell CO_2 generators specially designed for greenhouses, but household-style kerosene or gas heaters are also suitable. This apparatus needs no vent. The CO_2 goes directly into the room's atmosphere. A good heater will burn cleanly and completely, leaving no residues, creating no carbon monoxide. If a heater is not working correctly, most likely it will burn the fuel incompletely and create an odor. More expensive units have pilots and timers; less expensive models must be adjusted manually. Heaters with pilots can be modified by using the solenoid valve and timer.

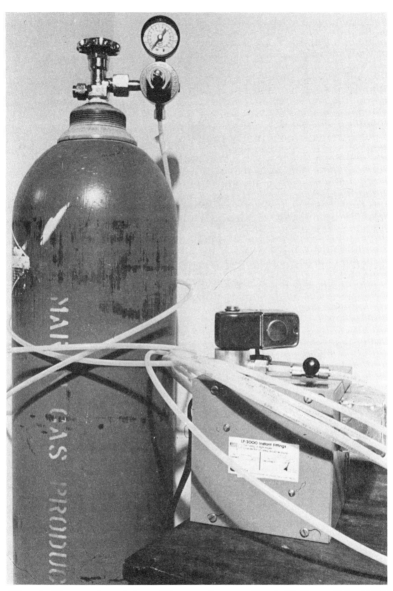

CO₂ tank with automatic regulation and flow control can more than double the growth in an enclosed grow room or greenhouse.

At room temperature, one pound of CO_2 equals 8.7 cubic feet. Remember that it takes only ⅓ of a pound of kerosene (5.3 ounces) to make a pound of CO_2. To find the amount of fuel you need to use, divide the number of cubic feet of gas required by 8.7 and multiply by .33. In our case, 5.6 cubic feet ÷ 8.7 × .33 equals .21 pounds of fuel. To find out how many ounces, multiply .21 by 16 (the number of ounces in a pound) to arrive at a total of 3.36 ounces, a bit less than half a cup.

Heaters do not specify the rate at which they burn fuel, but they almost always state the number of BTUs produced in an hour. To determine fuel use, divide the number of BTUs produced by 21,800. If a generator produces 12,000 BTUs per hour, it is using 12,000 ÷ 21,800, or about .55 pounds, of fuel per hour. However, only .21 pounds are needed. To find the number of minutes the generator should be on, divide the amount of fuel needed by the flow rate and multiply by 60. In our case, .21 (the amount of fuel needed) ÷ .55 (flow rate) × 60 equals 22.9 minutes.

CO_2 should be replenished every three hours during the light cycle, since it is used up by the plants and leaks from the room into the general atmosphere. Well-ventilated rooms should be replenished more often. It is probably more effective to have a generator or tank releasing CO_2 for longer periods of time, at slower rates, than for shorter periods at higher rates.

The simple process of supplying plants with CO_2 can increase the yield of any indoor garden considerably, so plan on decreasing the turnaround cycle of your garden — or raising the height of the ceiling.

Chapter Seven
The Super Grow Room

American marijuana cultivators are the most sophisticated, scientific farmers in the world. In just a few years they have mastered the techniques of breeding, hybridization, sinsemilla cultivation, and curing. They have doubled and redoubled the yield and potency of their crops. Although the media usually concentrate on outdoor "farmers," most outdoor growers these days raise only their own stash, or operate in a limited area using a controlled environment — i.e., a grow room. The high cost of marijuana and the risk involved in its cultivation have constantly challenged the cultivator to develop techniques that use space most efficiently. The potential for a high profit has also given growers the incentive and ability to experiment, and nowhere is this more apparent than in the indoor garden.

I have seen the super grow rooms (SGRs), and I believe. These growers have succeeded. SGRs are based on the idea of limiting factors. The plant's rate of metabolism — and subsequently its growth rate, maturation time and yield — are governed by environmental conditions that are linked together in a chain. Metabolism can proceed no faster than permitted by the five limiting factors: light, heat, water, nutrients, and carbon dioxide.

Super grow rooms meet these necessities, automatically or semiautomatically, by using timers that regulate irrigation, lighting, and CO_2 enrichment. Recently I had the pleasure of seeing two automated grow rooms. The first was lit naturally, with supplemental lighting from metal halides. The corrugated sheet-steel roof had been replaced with Filon, a transparent corrugated plastic sheet made especially for greenhouses.

Exec, as he wishes to be called, grows uniform commercial crops which vary according to the season. He has two growing areas: a starting room and a main growing area. His spacious starting room is divided into a germination section, lit by fluorescents, and a seedling section lit by two halides. Seeds are germinated in 4" pots and transplanted 10 days after germination into a 2½ quart container.

Exec has designed a planting schedule that matches each plant varieties' seasonal habits with day length. Here is his planting and control schedule:

In November, Exec starts equatorial seeds. He prefers a Nigerian-Santa Marta hybrid. He repots 10 days after germination, keeping the germination room lit 24 hours a day. The plants are removed to the large growing area about 3 ½ weeks after germination. This area is completely roofed with Filon, and has 10 halides for supplementary light. Total area is 1,000 square feet.

When plants are moved to the large growing area, they are repotted again, this time into 2-gallon containers. The lighting is set at 12 hours, to coincide with natural light. These lights burn only when the sun is out, so that suspicion is not aroused by the lit Filon roof.

To control the flowering period, Exec has strung rows of removable incandescents, each 100-watt light bulb illuminating about 9 square feet. For the next three weeks he turns these lights on for 1 minute (the minimum time on his short-range timer) every 90 minutes. This prevents the plants from starting to flower. Around the middle of January, he turns off the incandescents. A week later he turns the halides down to 10 hours, where they remain until the end of flowering. Exec claims to have had varieties that would not ripen until the light was down to 8 hours.

Around March 1 the new crop is planted. This time he uses either a Southern African-Afghani or Mexican hybrid. These plants are replanted around March 15 and then, around April Fool's Day, they replace the earlier crop, which is now ready to be harvested. Exec cuts the plants up and hangs them to dry in his starting room, which he now keeps entirely dark. He manicures them only after they are dry. Exec has a busy schedule transplanting the new residents of the growing area into 2-gallon pots. He keeps the halides on for 13–14 hours and then once again he uses his incandescents nightly, this time for two weeks, until about April 15, when he turns the halides down to 11 hours and covers the roof with long shades made from agricultural shading material. He manually opens and shuts the shades, closing them at dusk, as the lights go off, and opening them late in the morning as the lights come on. In late spring he sometimes uses only sunlight during the brightest part of the day.

These plants are only a month old. They are thriving in a near perfect environment, plenty of nutrient, water, and CO_2.

The same plants a month later.

On May 15 Exec plants another new crop. This time it is definitely an Afghani-Southern African, which flowers at 14–16 hours of light. By June 15 the Southern African-Mexican hybrid is ready, and the Afghani-Southern African plants are placed in the main garden. They are given only a natural-light cycle, and the halides supplement the natural light only on cloudy days. On July 15 they are shaded, to put them into harvest cycle, receiving no more than 14 hours of light. The plants are ready by August 30, and Exec replaces them with a Northern Mexican-Kush cultivar, or sometimes an Afghani-Kush hybrid that he's planted a month earlier. He uses flashing incandescents until September 30, when he lets the light cycle drop back to day length. The plants are ripe by December 15, a nice bit of Christmas cheer.

Exec gets four crops a year, uses a minimum of electric light, and is able to grow in a large area, arousing few suspicions regarding spinning electric meters.

He uses a propane heater during the cool months. This enriches the air with CO_2 while providing heat. At other times he uses CO_2 from a tank. During the hot months he uses a ceiling fan and several high-powered window fans, but even so, at times the room gets a little too warm for optimal growth. Cannabis grows fastest when the temperature ranges between the 60s and the 80s. If the temperature gets higher, photosynthesis stops; if it is lower, photosynthesis slows down.

With about 500 plants per crop, Exec has no time to water them. Instead, he has a drip emitter attached to each container, and each day he waters his plants by turning on a valve for a few minutes. First he determines how much water the average plant needs. Then, using a simple formula — amount required ÷ flow per hour × 60 — he arrives at the number of minutes needed for watering. His emitters flow at the rate of one gallon per hour (gph). If the plants require 8 ounces, 8 ÷ 128 × 60   3.7 minutes. When he is not around to take care of things manually, he estimates the plants' needs and then sets his short-term timer, which regulates a solenoid valve.

He adds soluble hydroponic nutrients and other fertilizers and minerals to the water solution several times a month.

The second garden I visited, administered by Elf, was lit entirely by halides and sodium vapor lamps. Elf's area totals about 225 square feet, of which 175 constitute growing space. He cultivates about 80 plants per crop and claims that he can grow five to six crops per year, but works at a more leisurely pace.

Elf too has a separate starting area. He can start a crop every two months, using the germination area for about one month before setting the plants in the main garden. Plants are started in 2½ quart containers; when they're moved, he transplants them to 1½ gallon containers.

Sometimes he starts from clones, which takes longer than starting from seeds, but is ultimately less effort since there are no males to deal with. Three weeks after the plants enter the main growing area, its light cycle is reduced to 13 or 14 hours from constant light. Six weeks later, the plants are ready to harvest.

Equatorial varieties take longer to mature, but Elf prefers them to the stuff he sells, so he has a growing room for his own stash. It is stocked with exotics.

Elf ventilates his area with two duct fans and open windows (which are covered to seal in light). CO_2 is injected into all three rooms from a CO_2 tank with a timer.

Elf waters his plants by hand, using a 5-gallon container and a ½ gallon pitcher. This takes less than an hour. At maturity the plants require about 1/2 gallon of water every four to seven days, depending on temperature. This saturates the container and partially fills the tray underneath it. Each container holds a mixture of vermiculite, perlite, Styrofoam, and foam rubber. Plants that are bigger than most receive extra water between irrigations. Smaller plants receive less water. He uses a combination of soluble fertilizers, and contends that his own urine, either fresh or fermented, is the best source of nutrients available. His plants were healthy and had no nutrient defiencies. But the taste...

Chapter Eight
Why Dope Gets You High

Aside from set and setting, the main factors in determining the quality and intensity of the high are the amount, and the particular ratio, of cannabinoids present in the material.

THE CANNABINOIDS

There are more than 40 known cannabinoids, but most of these occur in very small amounts and are not important to the high. The cannabinoids found in greatest quantity are THC, THCV, CBN, and CBC.

THC (tetrahydrocannabinol) is the main psychoactive (mind-bending) ingredient in marijuana, and accounts for most of the high. Actually THC is found in four or five variations with slight differences in their chemical structure. The variants have similar effects. THC occurs in all varieties of cannabis, in concentrations that vary from trace amounts to about 95 percent of all the cannabinoids present.

THCV (tetrahydrocannabivarin) is closely related to THC, and has been found in some varieties of Asian and African grass. Colombians have not yet been tested for THCV, but some varieties are likely to contain this substance. THCV seems to be much faster in onset and quicker to dissipate than THC, but its psychoactivity appears to be somewhat less than that of THC. THCV is usually associated with extremely potent grass.

CBD (cannabidiol) also occurs in almost all cannabis varieties in quantities that range from trace amounts to 95 percent of all the cannabinoids present. In its pure form it is not psychoactive, but does have sedative, analgesic, and antibiotic properties. CBD contributes to the high by interacting with THC to potentiate or antagonize certain qualities of the high. It appears to potentiate the depressant effects and to antagonize the euphoric effects. It also delays the onset of the high, but makes it last considerably longer. Terms such as "knockout," "sleepy," "dreamlike," and "contemplative" are often used to describe the high from grass with sizeable proportions of CBD.

CBN (cannabinol) is produced by the degradation of THC. Fresh samples of marijuana contain very little CBN, but curing, poor storage, or processing can cause much of the THC to be oxidized into CBN. When grass is pressed for shipping, the resin glands that hold and protect THC are sometimes ruptured, exposing the cannabinoids to air and increasing the rate of oxidation. CBN in its pure form has at most 10 percent of the psychoactivity of THC. CBN seems to potentiate THC's disorienting qualities, making one feel more drugged, dizzy, or generally untogether, but not necessarily higher. With a high proportion of CBN, the high may start well and then feel as if it never reaches its peak, and may not last long. Colombian grasses sometimes contain half as much CBN as THC.

CBC (cannabichromine) is inactive in its pure form, but is suspected of potentiating THC. Some tests made for CBD may actually have measured CBC, which is chemically similar.

THE EQUATORIAL THEORY

The ratios of cannabinoids found in different varieties of cannabis differ greatly. Generally, marijuana grown at the equator contains mostly THC, CBN, and THCV, with only traces of CBD. As the distance from the equator increases, the amount of CBD in relation to THC increases. At the 30th parallel (northern Mexico, Morocco, and Afghanistan), amounts of CBD and THC found in adapted varieties are about equal. Above the 30th parallel, cannabis plants are usually considered hemp.

But this is not a hard-and-fast rule. Within any macroclimatic area there are many microclimates, which may show extreme variations in environmental conditions. Since a patch of plants is adapted to the conditions in exactly the area where that patch is located, there may be major differences in the quality of adapted marijuana from several nearby stands. In the American Midwest, the content of CBD in samples of cannabis taken from escaped hemp (plants which had escaped from hemp fields) ranged from trace amounts to 7.1 percent; the THC content, from trace amounts to 2.3 percent. The high THC content indicates that there is potent marijuana growing "wild" in the Midwest. On the other hand, samples of hemp from India and Iran, two countries usually associated with good marijuana, contained (respectively) .11 and .18 percent THC and 2.4 and 1.63 percent CBD.

All this means that over many generations, each population of cannabis adapts to the particular conditions it faces. However, cannabis grown directly from tropical seeds will resemble its parents in growing habits and potency. First-and second-generation descendants will also reach a potency close to that of their tropical ancestors.

Evolutionary theories are predicated on the process of natural selection: that is, the plant that is more fit (for a particular environment) will be more likely to survive and reproduce. Just why the change in THC-CBD ratios occurs is unknown. However, America's marijuana growers, through selective breeding, have developed high-THC varieties adapted to the temperate environment.

The serious consumer faces two problems: ascertaining where the marijuana comes from, and determining the variety of seeds from which it was grown. Much of the grass now being imported was grown from top-quality seeds given to the grower by the dope exporter. For instance, the quality of Mexican has improved in recent years as Colombian and Southeast Asian seeds have been introduced to the area. Twenty years ago there was virtually no grass grown in Hawaii. Today, almost all of the grass grown there is descended from seeds recently imported to the islands from various sources. This becomes apparent when buds from different Hawaiian growers are compared. They differ in color, shape, size, as well as potency — factors determined in part by genetics.

Chapter Nine
Techniques for Preparing Soil

Each garden situation is unique: the soil's condition, the garden's size, its location, your commitment, and your personal preferences all play their part in determining which garden techniques you should use. Each technique affects the micro-ecology in its own way, and is useful for some set of conditions. Home gardeners can use techniques that are impractical for a farmer or a guerrilla planter. But all growers have the same goal when they prepare soil for planting: to create a soil environment conducive to the growth of a healthy, vigorous plant.

If you are already growing a vegetable garden, the chances are that your soil is in pretty good shape for growing marijuana. However, vegetable gardens may be a little acidic, particularly east of the 100th meridian. The soil should be prepared in much the same way as it is for corn, with the addition of lime to bring the pH close to neutral.

TILLING

Gardens that have not been planted recently (that is, within the past three or four years) require more work. It is best to begin preparing the soil in the fall before the first frost. This can be done using a spade or shovel. The ground is lifted from a depth of six or eight inches and turned over so that the top level, with its grass and weeds, becomes the bottom layer. Large clumps are broken up with a power hoe or roto-tiller. Conditioners such as fresh leaves, composts, mulching materials, pH adjusters, and slow-release fertilizers are added and worked into the soil so that they can begin to decompose over the winter. It is especially important to add these materials if the soil is packed, mucky, or clayey. Soluble fertilizers should not be added in the fall since they leach to the subsoil with heavy rains.

In the spring, as soon as the ground is workable, it should be turned once again. If it still feels packed, add more conditioners. If you are using manure or other organic materials, make sure that they smell clean and earthy and are well-decomposed. (Fresh materials tie up the nitrogen in the soil while they cure, making it unavailable to the plants.) Commercial fertilizers and readily soluble organics such as blood meal and wood ash are added at this time.

The ground can also be seeded with clover or other legumes. Legumes (clover, alfalfa, vetch, etc.) are plants which form little nodules along their roots. The nodules contain bacteria which live in a symbiotic relationship with the plant. As part of their life process, these bacteria absorb gaseous nitrogen from the air and convert it to chemical forms that can be used by the plant. During its life, the legume uses up most of the nitrogen, although some leaks into the surrounding soil. However, when the plant dies (or when any of its leaves die), its contents become part of the soil. The process of growing a cover crop and turning it into the soil is called "green manuring."

After the last threat of frost, at about the same time that corn is planted, the soil should be worked into rows or mounds, or hoed, and the seeds planted. If any concentrated fertilizer is added to the soil, it should be worked into the soil first, rather than coming into direct contact with the seeds.

The actual amount of tilling that a soil requires depends on its condition. Sandy soils and light loams may need no turning, since they are already loose enough to permit the roots to penetrate. Since turning breaks up the soil structure, damaging its ecology, it should be done only when necessary. These soils are easily fertilized using soluble mixes or by the layering technique described below. Soils which are moderately sandy can be adjusted by "breaking" them with a pitchfork: the tines are pushed into the ground and may be levered, but the soil is not turned. This is done about every six inches and can be accomplished quickly. Farmers can loosen sandy soil by disking at five or six inches.

Some gardeners mulch the soil with a layer of leaves or other materials to protect it from winter winds and weather. This helps keep the soil warm so it can be worked earlier in the spring. In states west of the 100th meridian, this is helpful for preventing soil loss due to erosion from dry winds. Soil often drains well in these areas and the soils' ecology is better served when they are not turned. At season's end, the marijuana's stem base and root system are left in the ground to help hold the topsoil. The next year's crop is planted between the old plant stems. Some gardeners prefer to plant a cover crop such as clover or alfalfa, which holds the soil while enriching the nitrogen supply.

LAYERING

Layering is another method of cultivation. The theory behind this program is that in nature the soil is rarely turned, but builds up, as layer after layer of compostable material falls to the ground. This material, which contains many nutrients, gradually breaks down, creating a rich humus layer over a period of years.

The layering method speeds up the natural process. Since gardens are more intensely cultivated than wild fields, new material is required to replenish the soil nutrients. Some gardeners sheet-compost: that is, they lay down layers of uncomposted material and let it decompose while serving as a mulch at the same time. Most gardeners, however, prefer to mulch with material that is already composted. The compost shrinks and builds the topsoil layer about an inch for every six inches of compost. After several years, the soil level will be raised considerably, and the top layers will constitute an extremely rich, porous medium which never needs turning. In order to prevent a spillover of the soil, gardeners usually construct beds which contain the garden areas. These are simply constructed with boards.

Layering is most successfully used on porous soils, especially sands, which contain little organic matter. It can also be used with clay soils, but experienced growers say that clays should be turned several times before the technique is used, or the first few harvests will be small.

Planting a cover crop such as clover will give the soil structure. As more compost is added, the clover will be covered and the new seed planted. The clover, with its nitrogen-fixing properties, remains as a permanent cover crop. When marijuana seeds are to be planted, a planting row can easily be tilled with a hoe. The clover protects the soil from sun-baking and resultant water loss, and makes it harder for weed seeds to get started.

Tilling and layering are basic methods, and are used in many variations. There are almost as many gardening techniques as there are gardeners. For instance, one gardener bought three cubic yards of topsoil and a cubic yard of composted steer manure. He mixed the material and filled raised beds with it to a depth of 1½ feet, creating an instant high-power garden. Another grower made compost piles in his raised troughs during the winter. By planting time the compost was complete and filled with earthworms. The beds became warm earlier, enabling him to plant sooner.

A Midwestern gardener uses marijuana as a companion crop in much the same way as Indians used corn: between the rows of marijuana, she planted string beans and squash. She didn't get many beans, and only a few squashes, but she points out that the beans gave the plants extra nitrogen, especially during the first six weeks, and that the broad squash leaves protected the soil from the hot August sun.

A gardener in Georgia had such a sticky clay soil that a shovel had once become stuck in it. He used a power auger to dig holes two feet deep and two feet wide, and filled them with a fertile mix of two parts sand, one part clay, three parts topsoil, and one part chicken manure. He claimed that his plants grew six feet in 2½ months.

Chapter Ten
Artificial Lighting

Greenhouse gardeners are used to harvesting summer crops one or two months earlier than their neighbors. Later in the season, the greenhouse environment allows them to harvest one or two months after other gardens have closed for the winter.

With just a small investment of time and energy, any greenhouse can be used to grow summer as well as winter crops nearly all year round, or until freezing temperatures kill summer plants.

In temperate zones the amount of light reaching sea level can vary considerably. In midsummer at noon on a clear day, I've recorded over 10,000 lumens at the 40th parallel. (A lumen is a measure equal to one footcandle per square foot.) In midwinter at noon, the same area received only 950 lumens. Fruiting plants require 2,000 to 3,000 lumens to produce, and 1,000 to 2,500 lumens to maintain life processes and slow growth. Non-fruiting plants, such as greens and root crops, generally require from 1,000 to 2,500 lumens.

Many greenhouses are already insulated and solarized to take advantage of the "greenhouse effect." The only thing that stops their plants from producing "summer" crops throughout the year is an adequate amount of light to support rapid growth.

Standard fluorescent fixtures are not the answer. The fixtures themselves block all sunlight that would reach the plant directly. Only ambient light, coming from the sides, gets through. The light is distributed unevenly, since the ends of a fluorescent emit considerably less light than its center area.

One way of increasing the efficiency of fluorescents is to build your own fixtures so that the spaces between the tubes are not blocked, and more direct light reaches the plants. Aluminum foil can be shaped to make reflectors, so that light that normally escapes from the top or sides of the tube is reflected downward. Use the dull side of the foil as the reflective surface. It reflects as much light as the bright side, but distributes it more evenly.

Lighting technology has increased the options of the home gardener. Besides the standard fluorescent, he/she can choose from

Very High Output (VHO) fluorescents, mercury vapor lamps, metal halide lamps, high-pressure sodium vapor lamps, and low-pressure sodium vapor lamps.

VHO fluorescents look just like the standard fluorescents, but use about three times the energy and emit about 2½ times the light. Although they are not as efficient as the standard lamps, they are much more convenient to use. Two of them replace a bank of five standard tubes. VHO tubes require a different ballast than do standard ones, but are the same size, so that more natural light is allowed to reach the garden. The tubes are positioned 6 to 12 inches from the tops of the plants.

A fruiting garden lit entirely by fluorescents requires about 20 watts per square foot of growing space. For example, a 4- × -8-foot garden (32 square feet) needs about 640 watts. At 72 watts for an eight-foot standard tube, this means that about nine tubes would be required. Most ballasts light pairs of tubes, so eight or ten would be the actual number. Eight tubes would be spaced at two per foot of width. A VHO fluorescent, on the other hand, uses 215 watts, so only three would be required. Even if four were used, there would be only one per foot of width.

Almost all gardens have bright spots and darker areas. Plants that require less light can be placed in the darker areas: for example, beneath the ends of the tubes, where the light emissions decrease dramatically.

Since greenhouse gardeners can count on some natural illumination, they do not need as many lamps. Almost all naturally lit gardens can get by on about 10 watts of electric light per square foot, so that the 4-by-8-foot garden in a greenhouse actually requires only half the number of tubes calculated above. Of course, if more light is used, the growth rate increases.

Fluorescents come in a number of different spectra, such as daylight, warm white, cool white, deluxe warm white, or deluxe cool white, as well as purple grow tubes. Many other spectrum choices are available. Each of these tubes is coated on the inside with a slightly different phosphor, which glows when it is activated by electric current. Each phosphor emits a unique spectrum of light, with the cool whites tending toward the blues, and the warm whites toward the reds. The term "deluxe" indicates that more red-emitting phosphors have been added. Although a garden using only one kind of tube will do fine, for best results the tubes should be mixed.

Fluorescent lights are adequate to bring plants into profuse ripe flowers. However, the light intensity goes down quickly as the distance from the tube decreases.

Grow tubes emit relatively high amounts of red and blue light. They were developed after it was discovered that chlorophyll uses red and blue light most efficiently. These lights were designed to approximate the photosynthesis (or chloroplast synthesis) curve. However, they emit less than 65 percent the light of other tubes (1,950 lumens). In experiments and informal inspections, I have observed that the responses of plants vary more with respect to the total lumens received than to the particular spectral pattern of the light. As long as the plants receive some light from each part of a broad spectrum, they will adjust and grow well. In practice, grow tubes do not work as well as other fluorescents.

Fluorescent tubes emit a lessening amount of light over the course of time. After a couple of years, they may emit less than 65% of their initial output. On-off cycles wear the tube out faster than continuous use.

Fluorescent lights use a ballast to convert electricity to a high-voltage, low-power current. Older ballasts were often insulated in PCBs, so it pays to buy new equipment, rather than risk a health hazard. Usually it is cheapest to buy a unit and rewire it onto the new frame. Every ballast has an easy-to-follow wiring diagram attached to it. The ballasts are the heaviest part of the fluorescent unit. For easy handling, it is best to separate the ballast from the lights. The ballasts can be placed on a board in a remote location, and the lights attached when the setup is in place.

A convenient way to light the garden is with a bank of U-shaped tubes, or with 8-inch round fluorescent converter fixtures. These units are designed to change a standard light fixture to a fluorescent one with a built-in ballast. A 2 foot- × -3 foot board can be used to mount standard fixtures, and then the fluorescents can be screwed in. They can also be hung independently from a rafter or frame, using a thin string, with each fixture attached to its own electric cord. I grew a garden in which I suspended these lamps so that they hung between the plants, not directly above them. This brought the lights very close to the flowers.

Metal halide lamps are the white-light street lamps used to illuminate everything from parking lots to night events. They are available in a number of wattages, but the two most convenient ones to use are the 400-and 1,000-watt sizes. They emit a mean of 32,000 and 92,000 lumens respectively, amd are slightly more efficient than a standard fluorescent. Mean lumens are used because the the lamp output changes as it wears out. 400-and 1,000-watt metal halide lamps have an initial output of 40,000 and 110,000 lumens respectively. A 400-watt metal halide lamp can be used as a supplementary source of light for an area of about 7 foot × 7 foot, or about 50 square feet. A 1,000-watt halide can provide illumination for about a 10 foot × 10 foot area, or a garden of about 100 square feet.

Plants seem to respond better to strong sources of illumination which are dispersed rather than to a moderate source which is emitted over a wider area. More light penetrates to the inner foliage. A metal halide's efficiency is increased when the halide shuttles back and forth, illuminating each garden spot brightly for a limited period of time. The area that the lamp can illuminate may be increased by about 30%, or the lamp can cover the same area with more light.

Metal halides promote vigorous growth. Fruiting patterns, which are somewhat slower using fluorescents, quicken; fast growth

This garden was illuminated with a metal halide lamp (front) and a low pressure sodium lamp (rear). Low pressure sodium is not ideal for marijuana but halides provide optimal intense light.

can be maintained even in midwinter. When I lived in an apartment, I grew tomatoes and herbs using halides in an unused hallway. I was eating juicy, ripe tomatoes 120 days after planting the seeds.

Sodium vapor lamps are the amber or orange-looking lamps used to illuminate streets and roads. Their spectrum is centered in the orange to red bands, but they emit some blue light. These lamps, too, come in 400-and 1,000-watt sizes. The 400-watt size emits 50,000 lumens initially, and has a mean rating of 445,000 lumens. The 1,000-watt lamp emits about 140,000 lumens initially, and about 126,000 mean lumens. It is about 1½ times as efficient as a fluorescent.

I have grown plants from seed using these lamps as the sole source of illumination, and the growth rate was about the same as with metal halides. Some gardeners claim that flowering and fruiting are increased because of the emphasis on the red spectrum. When the lamps are used as a supplemental light source, their spectrum becomes less important, since natural light will supply an adequately wide spectrum.

Low-pressure sodium vapor lamps emit an orange light that covers only a narrow portion of the visible spectrum (680–690 nanometers). They are very efficient. The largest size, a 180-watt unit, emits about 33,000 lumens, and is more than twice as efficient as a standard fluorescent. The lamp is encased in a three-inch-wide glass cylinder and consists of a U-shaped tube with the diameter of a neon light. It is powered using a ballast.

This lamp cannot be used as a primary source of light because plants grow stunted at first and eventually die. Low-pressure sodium lamps do work well as a secondary light source, though, and are an efficient way to increase the total number of lumens reaching the plant. They are especially good at brightening up dark spots in the garden.

Mercury vapor lamps also come in 400-and 1,000-watt sizes, and emit 12,800 and 47,700 lumens respectively. They emit a white light similar to a metal halide's, but are not nearly as efficient, so they should not be purchased new. If they are available used, though, they may be worth having.

For the most efficient use of any of these lamps, the reflectors should direct the light to the plants, not to the walls or ceiling of the room. Some commercial reflectors do not cover the lamps entirely, so that much of the light is directed horizontally rather than vertically or diagonally. Reflectors can be modified and customized using aluminum foil. It is easily held on by tying down with thin wire such as picture-hanging wire, which is not affected by the high temperatures.

Artificial light should be provided while natural light is present, so that the plants get as high-intensity a light as possible. If the garden is partially shaded, for instance, in the early morning or late afternoon, the lighting system may be used on a multi-cycle each day, being turned on and off several times, to supplement the natural light during the darker periods.

It is almost essential to put the lamps on a timer, so that they go on and off with regularity. As the natural light cycle changes with the seasons, the electric lights should be adjusted. During the late spring, supplemental lighting may be appropriate only at the beginning and end of each day. The lamps are generally not needed during summer. In early fall, they may be used during cloudy weather and at the beginning and end of the day. By late fall they may be used to supplement the weak sunlight all day, and may continue in this fashion until early spring.

Metal halide, low-and high-pressure sodium lamps, as well as accessories to shuttle the lights, are available from a number of horticultural supply companies.

Chapter Eleven
Harvest Time in India

The February 1980 issue of the International Cannabis Alliance for Reform newsletter contained an article which noted that marijuana was legal in three states of India. A year later I was on a jet headed for Bombay, India's largest city.

It's my policy not to carry contraband across borders. Soon after my companion and I were settled in a hotel, she became despondent about our straight condition. As we strolled toward an eatery, not a block from our expensive -for-India hotel, we were beckoned to by several teenage boys who, our sense of smell told us, were smoking hash or charas. Another firm policy of mine is to cop dope within 24 hours of hitting any city, just to keep in touch — but this was ridiculous. Within two minutes of our first touchdown in India we were sold some small dark brown balls (about⅛″ in diameter) which were very potent. One ball would break up nicely into a chillum. (That's an Indian pipe.) Since we had no chillum available, these people were kind enough to give us one. The balls were sold to us for about a rupee each (about 12½ cents at the time), which I am sure included an ample markup. Later we learned that the pipes are usually sold to Europeans for about half a rupee each.

Over the next two days we scored Goa and Kerala grass, or ganja as the Indians call it, as well as Kashmiri hash. The charas was good, but I still preferred the ganja. Ganja-charas joints were very potent.

Kerala is a state in southern India that is not traditionally known for ganja. Only since the '60s has cultivation spread to meet the demands of European tourists and the growing popularity of ganja among middle-class Indian college students and other young people. Goa was a colony of Portugal until it was annexed by India in 1961. After four centuries of colonization, the culture is as much Portuguese as Indian. It is a big tourist area, especially for young people, since it is relatively inexpensive and has good food and fine beaches. Hippies and hippie-influenced farmers grow some of the finest dope in all India here.

Government-regulated 10 acre ganja field in Kahandawa, India.

The three states I had read about that had legal cannabis were Madya Pradesh (MP), Orissa, and West Bengal. Orissa and West Bengal were further east, so we decided to start looking for the legal stuff in MP. Since I was determined to enter the fields officially, I decided to go to the capital, Bhopal. This is a state capital which, despite the context of Indian culture and design, would remind an American of any state capital: imperfect imitations of Federal architecture and a lot of bureaucrats.

On our way to the capital, as our train was passing through the town of Khandwa, my companion and I saw an astonishing sight: fields of marijuana growing right beside the railroad tracks. I wanted to dive out through the window.

When we reached the Department of Agriculture office, I explained that I was doing private research on marijuana and had published various works on the subject. We were ushered into the Director's office and were treated royally (even for India, where foreigners are generally treated with great respect). After being served tea, we explained that we had seen some fields in Khandwa. The Director told us that to his knowledge there was no ganja being grown in MP, but that he would check. A few hours later we return-

Typical Indian bud at harvest.

ed to his office; he informed us that there was indeed ganja growing in Khandwa, and complimented us on our ability to recognize it from a fast-moving train. (Aw, shucks...)

The Director told us that the government was also growing opium for medical use in Mandsaur, another town in MP. He wrote letters of introduction for me to the Assistant Directors of Agriculture in Mandsaur and Khandwa.

We decided to go to Mandsaur first. As soon as we'd arrived and presented the letter of introduction to the Assistant Director of Agriculture, he assigned us a guide. We were introduced to researchers working on developing poppies with better opium yields. They were also working on new harvesting methods. The fields had just been planted, so there were only some seedlings to be seen. "Come back in February or March. Then the plants will be flowering and we will be cutting the pods; then you can see all the different petals. We have single-and double-flowered, fringed, red, white, purple, and multicolored petals."

The next stop was an agricultural chemical company's research office, where I met one of the partners. He showed me an interesting hormone-type chemical, which he said could be used to

Soldiers guard two ox carts full of marijuana, bringing the harvest to the processing area.

cause sterility in pollen, and another which would decrease vertical growth. Then he took my companion and me back to meet his wife and children in their comfortable middle-class quarters. All of the people we met asserted that they'd never tried marijuana and were certainly not users. The agricultural chemist claimed that he'd tried it once, but it had made him go crazy for three days, following which he'd come down. He seemed very surprised when I told him that as a researcher I used it frequently, as did my female companion.

He explained that in India the only people who use ganja or charas are the poor and some of the followers of Shiva, who are ascetic religious wanderers and beggars. Middle-class people, he said, just don't use it. We explained that in America its use had become widespread despite government opposition, and that, in fact, many middle-class people all over Western Europe (and even in some parts of Eastern Europe) used cannabis. Later I learned that the use of pot has become epidemic among Indian university students, who are in fact primarily middle-class.

After spending a few days in Mandsaur, we started on our journey across Madya Pradesh to Khandwa. On the way we met an

The women stand in circles and strip all the vegetation from the stems and branches.

Indian family traveling with their niece, who was to be married in Uidaipur (a resort city just over the state line in Rajastan). I pulled out a Polaroid camera and took a few pictures of the traveling party. They had never seen an automatic instant camera before, and we were immediately invited to the wedding as guests and official photographers. After bidding farewell to the family, we backtracked to Khandwa.

It was lucky we had detoured for five days, because the harvest had just begun. It had been delayed because the strippers had gone on a short strike over a change in working conditions. Previously the plants had been stripped in the fields as they were cut. The workers peeled off the charas that accumulated on their hands, hid it, and later sold it. The new method was to bring all the plants to a central processing area where the workers could be more closely supervised. These women were the lowest-paid workers I heard of on my trip. They earned two rupees a day (about 25 cents at the time), which in India will buy you four cups of tea. Even the Excise Officers seemed embarrassed by the women's low rate of pay.

We arrived in Khandwa early in the morning. It was mid-November. After some telephone calls we were accommodated in

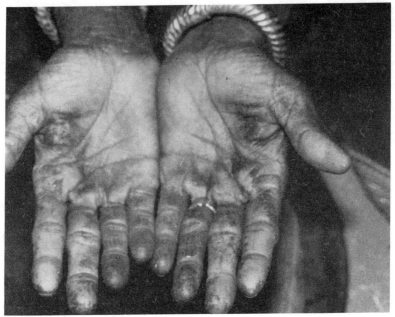

The hands of the women become sticky with resin.

the Circuit House, which is a modest but clean government-run hostel used primarily by government officials traveling on business. After some sleep, we visited the Director of Agriculture, who read our letter of introduction, then informed us that he was not empowered to admit us to the fields because they were not under his jurisdiction. They were administered by the Excise Department, he said. Later the same day, he informed us that we'd be able to visit the fields under the supervision of the Excise Department. Still later, two jeeps pulled up, one from the Department of Agriculture and one from the Excise Department. An assistant was assigned to us from the Department of Agriculture. We all piled into the jeeps and took off for the fields, which were about 10 miles outside of town. People stared at the strange sight of Europeans riding in government jeeps.

We entered the processing area, which was surrounded by chain-link barbed-wire fences, guarded by Indian Army regulars, and supervised by officials from Bhopal. We were introduced to the various officials, both from the D. of A. and the E.D., and to a consultant from West Bengal who is a successful farmer. Then we were introduced to local growers. Finally, just two officials escorted us out to the fields to let us investigate them at first hand.

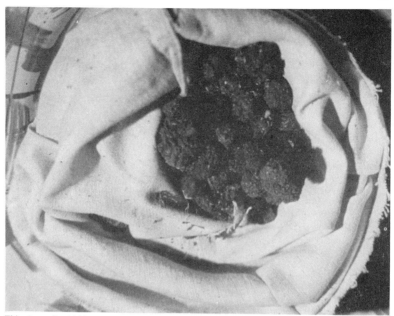

This charas (hashish) was scraped from the women's hands.

I saw two fields in Khandwa. One comprised five acres; the other, ten. The seeds had been sown about a foot apart in rows 2½ to 3 feet apart. The plants ranged from about five to ten feet tall, but most of them were between eight and nine feet. Rather than using a standard variety, or sowing each field with a particular variety (which would have been desirable for harvesting and quality control), the planters used mixed seed imported from Nepal. Some of the plants were past their prime, others were ripe, and one group had just begun flowering. The plants had not been sexed, and all the females were heavily seeded.

About 10% of the plants had died from a disease (probably fusarium wilt), which had attacked the plants suddenly and caused them to wilt and brown. The roots of infected plants were covered with a white growth. Apparently most plants had exhibited resistance to the infection.

After the marijuana is cut in the field, it is transported by oxcart, escorted by Indian government soldiers, to the processing area. It is unloaded and stripped by women standing in a large circle. They run their bare hands down each plant, leaving no vegetation on it. The leaves and buds fall into a large pile on the ground. The stems are discarded. After a pile builds to a height of about five

Workmen separate buds from the leaf. Buds are piled and allowed to ferment for three days from green to brown. Then they are dried.

inches, a concrete roller is used to compress the buds into tight clumps. The pile lies in the sun for several hours, and is then picked over by hand. The whole buds are placed in wicker baskets. A lot of shake is left on the ground. This consists of leaves (which deteriorate more quickly than the buds), seeds that are pressed from the buds, and glands that are knocked off. The shake is placed in a large pile to be destroyed under government supervision. When the strippers remove the vegetation it is green. The sun and the fermentation in the pile turn the buds brown. There was a distinct smell of ammonia coming from fresh piles, indicating anaerobic fermentation.

After the good buds are collected, they are placed out in the sun for further curing. Once again they are rolled and collected. In the evening, fifty-pound rocks are placed on the pile to compress it and to keep in some of the heat and moisture. Every few hours the buds are collected and repiled; each time, the shake is removed. By the end of the second day the grass is totally brown, and the compact clumps of buds look similar to Colombian. Almost all the leaf dries and is desiccated; the glands on the outer section are removed or broken. The marijuana has lost the aroma of freshness as a result of the evaporation and destruction of the mono-and di-turpines

The cement roller compresses the bud as it goes over the piles.

(essential oils) during processing. The quality of the cured smoke is perhaps 50% of the quality of the fresh material that we'd smoked. (Of course, other factors must be taken into account, since we selected our own fresh material.) During the sun-curing, some of the THC probably changes to CBN, which has only 10% of the potency of THC. However, all the remaining THC is stable, since it is compressed into an air-and light-free clump. It can be transported roughly with little further deterioration. Marijuana dried in the American fashion is very fragile and cannot stand rough treatment.

During this tour, I asked the Excise Officers whether they wished to improve the quality of the ganja. They replied that only the poor and the religious smoke it, that these people use it to drown their sorrows, and that it makes them lazy. If it were more potent they would just get lazier. The Officers seemed unconcerned that as a result of using mixed seed, there was no quality control.

After allowing me to take a few pictures and to pick a few buds (which we used to show American drying techniques to the Officers), our guides took us back to the Circuit House.

The next morning, we had an Indian breakfast with the Chief Excise Officer, who was also staying at the Circuit House. It included yogurt, chapatti (flat bread), fruit, cauliflower in a light curry

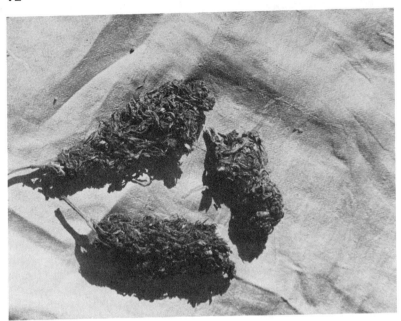

Buds after curing.

sauce, and tea with milk. I explained that in the U.S., marijuana prohibition was a total failure. By our government's own reckoning, it was seizing only 10% of the weed on the black market. More people than ever were smoking. Large non-legal groups had been formed to circumvent the ban on importation, and the domestic cultivation industry was quickly capturing the high-priced end of the market.

The Officer was interested. According to the Single Convention on Narcotics and Dangerous Drugs, which India signed in 1964, that country has committed itself to making cannabis cultivation or sale illegal within 25 years of the date of signing. If this happens, a large legal industry in India will be handed over to black marketeers. A source of revenue to the government will be eliminated, and legal farmers and businesspeople will be put out of work. Making the herb illegal will result in a new police and civil bureaucracy, and a net economic and social loss to the Indian federal and state governments. (There is already a thriving black market in charas and high-quality grass in every state of India.)

After breakfast we returned to our room. A few minutes later, there was a knock at the door, and the two Excise Agents barged in. One of them was carrying a load of ganja in his cupped hands. He put it on the table, explaining that it was a present for us. This was

Group photo of author with government officials.

the first time a government official had ever barged into my room to give me drugs. He noticed a chillum, and asked whether we knew how to use it. We explained that we preferred to roll joints, but he insisted that we both become proficient in the use of the chillum. We had not yet gotten the chillum hand positions down, so he instructed us. It must have been a rare event for him to see a woman smoking. He looked at the grass that we'd dried, and said that Indians would not smoke such green material. Obviously they were suffering from New York Syndrome.

Later that day, a convoy of five jeeps arrived at the Circuit House to take us back to the fields. More officials and researchers had joined the party and wished to meet me. I took a series of pictures of them, then headed back to the fields to shoot more pictures, look at the plants, and do a bit more picking. This time I penetrated deeper into the field so that all I could see around me was cannabis. I picked some choice buds.

When we got back, the women were being directed in scraping their hands. They all sat in a straight line as a supervisor with a long stick directed the operation. The little balls of charas were collected and placed in a muslin bag, which was sewn closed and signed by several Excise Officers. It was to be taken to Bhopal to be destroyed. One officer said to me, "Look but do not touch."

The officials conjured up a saddhu (religious pilgrim) to smoke with the author and companion.

One of the Excise Officers asked me what a field like this one would be worth in the United States. I judged the field's quality to be that of medium-to high-grade Colombian, which in the U.S. would be worth about $700 (or 5600 rupees) per kilogram. There were about 2300 kilograms per acre; if there were ten acres, I said, that would be about 16 million dollars, or 120 million rupees. He began giggling. In India this ganja sold in the shops for half a rupee per gram, or about $65 per kilo. The government buys the wet grass from the farmers for about $2 per kilo and sells the dried cured material to the stores for $30 per kilo. Cultivation other than by license is illegal, as is possession of more than 20 grams.

After the workers had left the area, there were about 20 Excise Officers left. As the sun went down, they conjured up a Saddhu, a devotee of the god Shiva (whose adherents use ganja to attain enlightenment). The Officers had us smoke from the chillum with the Saddhu. None of them smoked with us. Since this was a hick town, the Officers needed something to keep themselves amused, and we were the early movie.

After a while, the party broke up and we went back to the Circuit House. We left for New Delhi the next day, carrying with us some of the finest legal grass in India — our American-dried grass, which I'd picked in the fields myself.

Chapter Twelve
Medical Marijuana

I was recently given a marijuana cigarette by a cancer patient who received his stash from the Federal government. This was my first opportunity to test medical marijuana grown for the government.

The government sponsors a research program at the University of Mississippi, and distributes the marijuana grown there both for research and for medical prescriptions from all over the United States. The marijuana is supplied in the form of standard-sized cigarettes, rolled on a cigarette-rolling machine. These cigarettes look innocent enough, except that the ends are dark green rather than brown.

Using a small-bladed knife, I dissected the cigarette lengthwise, along the seam. The contents consisted of sunleaf, leaf stems, and a few growing tips, all in the vegetative state. They were yellow or brownish green.

Visually comparing the marijuana from the joint with the pictures in some standard reference works from my library, I found that the marijuana looked like early-harvested lower plant parts. This material is commonly discarded or sold for under $100 per pound.

I gathered a panel of daily smokers who prefer sinsemilla, sometimes grow their own, but have been known to smoke Colombian. There was enough marijuana for two joints. After passing the lit sticks around, I elicited some comments:

"This is foul and evil stuff."

"Like the first bag of pot I bought — through Rolling Stone."

"Not good-tasting, but I feel it."

"Leafy, harsh, one-quarter the potency of sinsemilla. The kind of pot you smoke when you're going cold turkey from nicotine."

"Wow. This is really harsh, hot, and dry-tasting."

A legal marijuana cigarette.

"Hey, this stuff tastes a lot better than government pot!"

I found the joint to be very harsh, as harsh a sunleaf as I have tasted. This is probably because of the small stems which are cut fine and mixed with the leaf. The pot was relatively strong, though, especially for leaf from immature plants.

I've noticed, however, that the buzz that I get from an immature plant has different qualities from the high produced by mature flowers. Perhaps the plant produces a slightly different analog in the flowers. The government-sponsored researchers, by the way, decided not to use flowers because they contain too much resin and gum up the rolling machine, which was manufactured to be used with tobacco.

The University grows only one variety, a Mexican, for medical use. This variety was arbitrarily chosen as the sole source of medical marijuana because Dr. Carlton Turner, the former director of the government-funded, marijuana-growing research project at the University of Mississippi, and the researchers associated with the program felt that the cannabinoid mix in each variety would need to be filed as a new investigative drug and that the plant components were so complex that starting on more than one variety was unrealistic.

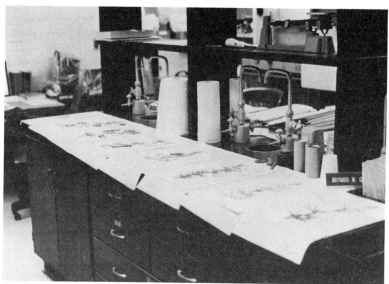

A legal, government-issue joint was opened and compared to two grades of lower leaf. The government pot looked worse and smoked harsher.

Just as with prescription drugs, slight variations in the formulas of different varieties may affect patients and symptoms in different ways. One variety of marijuana may be better to relieve the symptoms of chemotherapy, another for radiation therapy, and still another for glaucoma.

The University has not investigated other possible medical uses of marijuana. For instance, the long-term effects of marijuana on blood pressure have not been looked into.

Patients who rely on the government are getting a rew deal. The pot they receive is not worth more than $5 to $20 per ounce on the open market. If they want a better grade, they're not permitted to purchase it. The government's getting a raw deal too. The cultivation program costs taxpayers much more per ounce than the patients would have to pay on the open market for the pot they receive. The government certainly pays more than $6.25 per ounce, the cost of pot at $100 per pound.

Perhaps the government should buy pot from independent cultivators. If the government bought leaf from growers, this would be the first subsidy for marijuana cultivators. So many farmers would line up to supply the government with pot that a crash program would be have to be inaugurated to find suitable recipients. There might be cancer-glaucoma screening clinics so that the shake surplus wouldn't have to be stored in special grass silos. Perhaps the government could distribute the surplus to underdeveloped countries such as Colombia... Of course, there would still be the problem of what to do with the buds.

Chapter Thirteen
Growing Pot Indoors with Natural Light

Most articles and books on growing marijuana discuss methods of cultivating the plant indoors under artificial light or planting outdoors. But there's another alternative: growing indoors using natural light.

Porches and windowsills, skylights and translucent roofs, greenhouses and lean-tos are all possible garden sites for natural-light cultivation. Any area which can supply the plants with five hours of direct sunlight during the peak of the growing season (June/July) can support vigorous growth and lush, healthy plants. (When marijuana does not get enough light it will grow an elongated stem and small leaves.)

Southeastern and southwestern exposures provide the most sunlight, followed by southern, eastern, and western exposures. But even a northern exposure is adequate if the garden is given supplemental light from an incandescent grow bulb or a small fluorescent unit.

Growing under natural light is easy and requires little equipment: just a container, planting mix, and fertilizer. Although most natural-light gardeners grow only a few plants, hefty crops can be grown in greenhouses, under skylights, and in large windows.

DETECTION

Detection is the main problem faced by natural-light gardeners. It's hard to explain to a cop that you never noticed those familiar seven-fingered leaves growing in your living-room window. But plants can be hidden by using curtains, plastic film, or crystal paint (which is sold in tropical fish stores to decorate tanks). Make sure that the plants cannot be seen in silhouette at night. They can also be placed at a distance from the window, or below it, to keep the garden invisible from outside.

Don't forget that in some cities and towns, cops waste taxpayers' money by searching upper-story apartments from street level with binoculars.

STARTING

To get started, just fill a container with potting soil or mix from your local nursery or garden center. Some gardeners mix these in a two-to-one ratio with perlite or vermiculite.

Seeds can be planted in individual pots, in flats, or in large containers. Fast-growing marijuana plants will outgrow small pots or flats very quickly, and will eventually need a three-to five-gallon container. Gardeners can choose the most vigorous seeds for transplanting.

Another method "postage-stamp gardeners" often use is to plant several seeds in one larger container, and to thin them as they grow and begin to crowd each other. Both methods work well.

SUPPLEMENTAL LIGHT

Gardeners who don't have an adequately lit area for cultivation can use artificial light as a supplement. The easiest method is to use a grow bulb, which fits in an ordinary socket. Clamp fixtures will hold the lights in convenient positions.

Fluorescent units provide a more efficient source of light, since they produce more light per watt and come in a variety of spectra. As a supplemental source, any white light spectrum such as cool white, warm white, daylight, natural white, vita-lite, optima, or merchandiser white will do. Different spectrum tubes can be used together so that a broader spectrum is provided.

The amount of supplemental light required varies with the amount of natural light the garden receives. An unobstructed northern exposure requires no more than 10 watts of fluorescent light during the winter. But more light promotes more vigorous growth.

Let's say you're growing in a northern window that is $1\frac{1}{2}' \times 3'$, or a total of $4\frac{1}{2}$ square feet. You need 45 watts. Two 2-foot fluorescent tubes use about 40 watts, or a fraction less than 45. Usually lamps used for supplemental lighting need to be on for no more than eight hours per day, so they can be used during daylight to attract the least attention. However, they may be ineffective if used in this way, since the plants may be getting as much energy from the strong daylight as they can use.

In Amsterdam, this simply constructed wood frame greenhouse covered with polyethylene film is an inexpensive way to provide shelter for plants.

This greenhouse was very tall. The plants grew to full height. The fan is used to recirculate air.

GROWTH AND FLOWERING

Spring or early summer is the best time to start marijuana indoors, but it can be started at any time of the year. During the winter the plants' growth will be slower, and the leaves smaller, because of the weaker light.

The female marijuana plant flowers when the days grow shorter; it chemically monitors the number of hours of uninterrupted darkness. The male may flower irrespective of the light cycle. If you don't illuminate the growing area, the plant will flower in the fall. However, if the lights are turned on at night, the female plant will not flower. It will continue to grow new leaves and branches, will show a spurt of energy each spring, and will live for several years.

If you wish to assure darkness to induce flowering, you can put the plants in a closet at sundown each day and bring them out each morning. They will flower within a few weeks. After flowering, if you cut off all the bud material, but allow some leaf to remain, the plant may begin to grow again.

Lighting Chart

Use tubes from Column A in 1-1 or 1-2 ratio with any tube from Column B

Column A	Column B
Daylight	Natural White
Cool White	Merchandiser White
Decorator Blue	Soft White
	Warm White Deluxe
	Cool White Deluxe

Chapter Fourteen
Sinsemilla Seeds

In the past two growing seasons the quality of sinsemilla has gone down considerably. This is the result of growers' breeding to please the market: a situation somewhat analogous to that of tomato breeders. Both feel that regardless of the quality of the product they put out, it will sell as long as it is cosmetically appealing. Both have other market considerations as well. Tomato growers want a fruit that ships well, even if it tastes like cardboard. Commercial marijuana growers want plants that come in early, no matter what the quality of the high. They want the pot to be odoriferous, with thick, compact buds. And, in fact, the market does seem to respond more to these factors than to the quality of the high.

Breeders have been developing just the plant for the farmer's needs: the indica hybrids crossed with Hindu kush, Southern African, or even a Mexican. The three primary factors that growers look for are heavy yield, compact plants, and (most of all) early maturation date. Between the weather, the thieves, and the law enforcers, growers would rather have an inferior-quality plant to sell than none at all. The result has been sinsemilla that is not as potent, nor qualitatively as satisfying, as the commercial sinsemilla that was available in 1980–81.

Part of the blame clearly rests on the political situation, which has forced growers to seek earlier and earlier varieties. Yet there is no reason for growers and breeders to sacrifice exactly what is sought from the marijuana plant — the high.

One of the important features of breeding programs run by the growers themselves is their way of choosing males for breeding. The grower typically takes elaborate care in choosing his/her females, assessing many factors. But choosing the male for cross-breeding is more difficult. How can one choose a male for the quality of the female buds its progeny might produce?

Very carefully. First, make a list of factors that are important to you. Then see which of these can be determined in a male plant. These might include maturity date, average height, branching characteristics, and — as a matter of fact — the high. Though they're not the most desirable, males do get you high. They should be tested for their relative strength.

If you have the space, try growing some longer-maturing varieties, at least for breeding. Though the females will probably not mature outdoors until the end of October, and sometimes even later, the males can be used to pollinate other plants. The first generation (F_1) will be pretty uniform. Subsequent generations will vary more, showing different characteristics of their ancestors. By carefully selecting these plants, you can eventually develop a fairly uniform variety.

One way to speed up breeding is to cross only female plants with each other. Normally, of course, this is impossible. Female plants usually produce only female flowers. Hermaphrodites, which are primarily female and produce some male flowers, are usually culled to prevent seeding, because their progeny would carry genetic information that could produce male flowers on female plants.

However, male flowers can be induced on female plants by using a substance called gibberellic acid. These male flowers will have only the information that their mothers had. They will not carry hermaphroditic genes. They will produce only females, since they have only female chromosomes.

Gibberellic acid is a natural plant hormone whose effects were first observed on rice plants, which were infected with a fungus that produced it. They grew elongated stems and also showed sexual abnormalities. Gardeners and nurserypeople now use the substance to grow enlarged flowers and elongated stems, and to alter the gender of plants. It has never been observed to have any effect on animals, and is considered safe. It is available in spray cans at many nurseries and garden supply stores.

To use it, spray the branch on which you wish to induce production of male flowers. As soon as you see any indication that male flowers are forming, cut the branch from the plant and place it in a very moist medium or in a jar of water. (Change the water daily or aerate it with a gentle bubbler.) Either way, fertilize it with a very dilute solution and use a rooting/fungicide powder.

Soon the buds will develop into flowers. Make sure that the branches are in separate draftless spaces, so that the pollen drops directly onto a sheet of paper placed under the branch.

You can cross a plant with itself without diluting any of the genetic material. This is very important when you have an unusual plant, or a plant with an unusual characteristic that you wish to preserve. Even if the gene for that characteristic is recessive, it will still appear in the offspring. If the plant has only recessive genes for a particular characteristic, and you cross the plant with its own pollen, then all the new plants will have that characteristic. If the gene is dominant and the plant also carries a recessive gene affecting that characteristic, then it will appear on about three-fourths of the plants. (One-fourth of the plants will carry only the desirable gene; half will carry a mixed pair; one-fourth will not have the dominant gene at all.) If the gene is only partially dominant, then some plants will show characteristics somewhere between those of the two competing genes.

You can also cross two females which are easier to analyze. Since both plants are female, both parents may be compared with other females, eliminating guesswork.

Breeding is not quite this simple, of course. Frequently a characteristic is controlled by more than one gene. In other cases, there may be a "trigger gene" that turns the desired gene off and on. While breeding for one factor, you must watch the others as well, or the quality of the buds may decline.

However, the results of a well-managed breeding program can be quite rewarding: heavier-yielding plants, greater potency, and earlier maturity.

Chapter Fifteen
Morocco Adventure

One day while I was perusing my *High Times* magazine, I noticed advertised tours of Amsterdam and Morocco. I had been to Amsterdam several times and certainly did not need a tour of that city, but a tour of Morocco intrigued me. It is one of the hash-making countries, but its products were not known for their high quality. On the other hand, I had never seen commercial hash-making. I called the number in the ad and wrote for the brochure. The next day the brochure arrived in the mail. It had been sent to me before I requested it.

After speaking with Ray, the tour proprietor several times, we made arrangements that I would pay half the airfare and he would subsidize my tour. As it turned out, he was going to take a loss on the tours for 1982 because I was the only person who signed up. This is not necessarily an indication of Ray's abilities or the attractiveness of the tour, but simply that Americans are no longer traveling, especially out of the country. In fact, in 1980 when I went to Europe and Asia, I met only one American couple traveling strictly for pleasure. This is not to say that I didn't meet Americans, but there were all out of the states for one business reason or another, and as a traveler, when you say you're from America, people in different countries always ask "What happened?" "Where are all the Americans?" and they're usually very cordial. I guess that they thought that they didn't like Americans when instead they were left just the Germans, Japanese, and Australians who seemed to be the main travelers these days, they found that they really did like Americans. Anyway, when I signed up for Ray's tour, I didn't realize that I was the only person. Later on, before we traveled, he told me that his efforts to interest travelers had come to naught.

Ray flew to Morocco several weeks before I arrived during the last week of August. He met me at the airport and we took a bus into town. When we arrived in Casablanca, Ray had me drag my suitcase for 15 blocks to the hotel. As usual, it was a sunny day; it was lucky that my luggage had wheels or else I might have passed out right then. The hotel that Ray had planned for us was booked up, so I dragged my suitcase another few blocks before arriving at a tourist-class hotel. The next day we left for Fez, which is an all-day train-ride from Casablanca.

From Fez we took a Mercedes taxi , which normally seats 5 but which I immediately learned seats 7 or 8, from the foothills into the mountains. As soon as we were in the taxi, one of our fellow passengers proceeded to make a hashish joint. He made this using tobacco from a Marlboro cigarette and a higher grade Moroccan hash — some of the darkest to be seen.

The last 30 kilometers to Ray's friend's house were accomplished by hitching on the side of the road, since the taxi route did not go into the mountainous terrain. Luckily, somebody recognized Ray, turned around his Datsun pickup and gave us a ride up to cafe in Ray's friend's town. Soon after I entered the truck, I was sitting in the cab with the driver and Ray was in the back when a woman sneaked into the cap with the help of the driver, unseen by neighbors. As we drove off she ducked below window level so she couldn't be seen. It was obvious that she and the driver were planning a tryst at the end of the ride. This was the first example I saw of relationships between men and women in Morocco. If the woman was seen by her neighbors, her entire life might be ruined, and she might be in physical danger.

Ray's friend was happy to see him and greeted me effusively, and we sat down to a few cups of mint-flavored tea. I asked Ray's friend, Boummedeine, how his fields were. He said that they had all been harvested, that all the neighbors fields had been harvested, and as far as he knew, all the hashish plants in the whole area and country had been harvested. I was a little disappointed. After the tea, we proceeded up the mountain to Boummedeine's house in his Mercedes. From the patio, there was a beautiful view of where the fields had been; we could see the stalks from the plants that had been collected and we could also view the plants drying and in the storehouses.

But we saw not one, decent, harvestable plant. Ketama, the main city in the area, is 10 miles away. It is in the center of the Reef mountains and is probably the hash-making capital of Morocco. On the other hand, it's also a main road for tourists going to resorts who pass through the town. Tourists who stop at the government-run hotel, in season, have a splendid view of the hash plants growing not 20 feet from the road. Some young local men hang out in the hotel bar partly in the hopes of having profitable encounters with Europeans, to drink beer, or to watch Spanish television, which is a lot more interesting than Moroccan.

The second day that we were in the Ketama area, we met a guy who told us that his fields were still up. He said that it would be most convenient to have a vehicle to get to them. We made arrangements to go the next day. Ray's friend's or Ray himself misunderstood the arrangements and while we had arrived at the farmer's house, we had to hike to the fields. It was miserable. The sun was beating down on us, dehydrating us. Ray, who was a heavy cigarette smoker, had to stop every 15 minutes to rest, and this uphill trek went on for over an hour and half. When we got to the fields, there was nothing worth seeing. All the plants had been cut down. The only things standing were dried out runts.

We walked on a little further to a hash-making area located in an incompleted house and could see the road not 100 feet away. Going down the hill, Ray mentioned that he thought about renting a car, but had decided not to because of the expense which I would have had to help repay since he was working on a limited budget. He had decided not to because his friends had assured him of their services. The walk down the hill was, of course, easy on the heart, but steep slopes get to my knees and after an hour, between the dehydration and the stress on unused muscles, I was exhausted.

The farmer did not appreciate the walk either.

At the end of the hill he started to make his sales pitch for hashish, hash oil, and ganja, and Ray acted irate at the suggestion that we buy something from this guy that had caused him such a misadventure. But the guy had just spent 3 hours, which he'd not anticipated. He'd showed us the hospitality of his fields and home and at the end of a half-day's work was being left with no money. He demanded money for taking us up. Ray would not bargain with him or even discuss it and just kept walking straight ahead, ignoring his requests. Finally, the farmer practically begged and implored Ray to come to the house and just buy a token amount — a few grams. Ray refused.

The farmer was still haggling with Ray. Ray pulled out a 100 Durham note worth about $16.00 and threw it at him. The guy took it but was insulted. He didn't really want the money for the tour. He wanted Ray to buy even $3 or $4 worth of hash. Ray had made an enemy for life.

We spent the following day waiting for Ray's friends to take us on a tour of the countryside to try and find some pot plants. But his friends never had the time, or were un willing to take us around.

We were staying in a room overlooking a field that Boummedeine owned. The room was furnished like thousands of others in
the area that cater to foreign visitors and exporters. Around the cir-
cumference of the long, narrow room, in this instance a long, narrow space, was a 2 foot deep by 30 inch wide foam bench covered
with assorted cloth. The walls, which had been painted years ago,
were decorated with assorted memorabilia left by the other visitors.
The toilet was outside down the stairs and consisted of a squat pit,
not too sanitary. We ate outside with Boummedeine and his
brothers and cousins who all worked together. The food consisted
of flat, soft breads and meat stew, primarily lamb.

The patio was also the main living room although it was getting
chilly in the evenings. The interior of the house, which I never
entered, consisted of an inner courtyard with rooms off of it. This
was the women's area. Unless they were in the fields, they were
always behind the doors of the house, working.

There was very little public interaction between men and
women. It seemed to me that they lived in two separate cultures.
Boummedeine had two wives and his father, now deceased, had
four, now widows who lived in a house 100 yards from him. All of
the women worked the fields, helped to cook and rear the children.
The men made deals and sat around. I never saw men in this family
working hard at manual labor.

The next day, after considerable thought, I decided to move to
the hotel in town. Although I am not shocked or upset by primitive
conditions, I see no reason why I should experience them if I didn't
want to. I do appreciate a hot shower and electricity, which went
off at midnight until morning. On the other hand, I did not wish to
upset Boummedeine or his brothers. Ray told me that Boummedeine certainly did understand, that he had spent some time in
Amsterdam and realized that Europeans had different
expectations.

Around midafternoon, I checked into the Ketama Hotel. I put
my belongings in my room and went out to the bar to see what was
going on. I hadn't eaten so I ordered some food when one of the
patrons approached me and said "You didn't find any hashish at
Boummedeine's. We have a whole field."

I said "Really? Is it green or brown? I have already seen lots of
harvest fields, but I want to look and photo one that is still up."

One of the two guys talking to me said,"It's half gone, but
there are a lot of green growing plants around."

A marijuana plantation in the Reef mountains of Morocco.

"Are you sure that they are not harvested?"

"Yes."

"Well, when can I seem them?"

"Right now."

"I haven't eaten all day. I have to wait for my sandwich and also I have to clean and adjust my camera."

"Okay."

I bought them beers, 8 ounce Heinekens at $2.50 a bottle. The cheese sandwich rapidly disappeared from my plate and after getting my camera gear ready we started out. It was about 3:30 so that there was not that much good daylight left. Our Audi navigated the main road, then a side road and pretty soon we were on a long winding road in desolate, dry country. It looked like southern California. We passed over outcroppings and there was no sign of any habitation. Finally we came to a large working farm but just continued.

I was getting nervous. True enough, the guys were friendly, had given me no reason to be the least bit paranoid, and had not made any kind of threatening remarks, but as the ride extended to forty minutes, I began to feel insecure. By this time we were traveling up a mountain pass. The car followed the road's 90 degree turn and we came to a most amazing sight.

Moroccan plants are grown close together and have a single flowering top on a slender stem.

A whole mountain and valley was spread out before us. And the entire area, the valley below and the terraced mountain were covered with hashish plants. People were working in the fields harvesting the plants by hand using scythes to cut them. The scene looked like a van Gogh painting brushed with broad strokes of deep colors — the greens, the colorful women's clothing, and the tan browns and grey tones from harvested fields and boundaries.

This was extensive. There are five villages within the valley and each of them receives its entire income from hashish.

We were right at the entrance to the whole valley. The whole panorama spread before us was perfect for photography, and the light was still bright enough for some shots of the fields. My two new friends used the house right at the foot of the road. I set up my camera and used a couple of rolls of film. Then we went through the village in the valley to reach the fields. Each terraced area was farmed by a different family. The terraces in the valley had soil which was rich and fertile, collecting the runoff from the mountain. The terraces followed the land's contours. As the land rose from the valley, its topsoil layer thinned, and the plants which grew on it became shorter, with pale green leaves and yellowed lower branches. The colas were thinner. Finally in the upper gardens, stretched

The Moroccan flowering tops are sparse with buds.

The harvest is set out to dry.

thin against the mountain's slope, the farming became even more marginal.

The farmers had different techniques. Most farmers planted over 40 seeds to the square foot, but some of them sowed as few as 10 or 12 to the square foot. Fertilization techniques differed also. Most farmers added little or no fertilizer. But some of them used quite a bit. Their plants were much larger and more vigorous, but they were later maturing. All the plants seemed to be from the same variety and the farmers did not seem to be too interested in the genetic backgrounds of their plants. This is not to say that I expected them to be using altogether scientific breeding techniques, but they used no selection process in choosing seeds.

The village was all mud paved, but it was the dry season and the small houses (which we would consider cottages) had small courtyards and sometimes an inner yard. These were not well-to-do people, but more like yeoman farmers.

Up close, the fields showed the results of different cultivation techniques. Some of the plants may have weighed a quarter-pound dry, but most of them weighed a fourth of that. As I mentioned, the plants are grown very close together and because of that they do not branch much. Each plant grows a single main stem and a thin cola.

Soon the light became unusuable and as we walked back to the house we smoked some hash and talked about ourselves and our societies.

After an hour or so, when it was completely dark,we drove through the mountainous roads back to the hotel. The moon was nearly full and the land reflected the light with a unique luminosity. The rocks and boulders were surrounded by halos, and the few plants growing in the dry land cast dark shadows as they absorbed the moon rays.

At the hotel, I found Ray waiting for me, very concerned. His friends had told him that one of my new acquaintances was crazy and the other merely malevolent. Ray was happy to see me alive, and when I told him that what I had found, he was relieved that his tour was saved from disaster. Now he need not tear his hair out searching for live fields.

I introduced them all and then our farmer friends suggested that we return to the fields that night. Ray had arranged for us to go to a wedding the same day, so we postponed the return to the fields for two days.

I got another cheese sandwich at the bar, and with some fruit that I had purchased at a local market, retired to my room.

Later that evening I returned to the bar, which was filled by members of a French tour traveling overland to one of the resorts. Some of the local young men were flirting with a couple of heavier ladies.

The next day, Ray came over to use my shower, which he found better than the portable solar shower he was using, which was a black polyethylene plastic bag with a shower head. Then we went to the local cafe, where we waited awhile and then walked the mile up the hill to Boummedeine's house. At the house we waited for several hours for friends to show up and give us a ride into the next town. No one showed so we decided to walk the 6 miles over the mountain pass to the next town. The walk was beautiful. For the most part, the only sounds that we heard were nature's. The wind blowing steadily created a thousand whistles, which changed tones ever so slightly from moment to moment, so that our ears were never bored. The music had the same soothing effect as a drone, the constant tone found in classic Indian music and the Irish bagpipe. The birds' different melodies suspended hundreds of notes in mid-air. The sounds that we made as we walked over these well-worn shortcuts, over the rocks and into the new valley, gave the natural symphony a steady beat. From the top of the pass we could see two villages and hundreds of acres terraced so that all the mountain became valuable farmland.

By the time we arrived at the wedding, the ceremony had taken place; once again Ray had messed up. The problem was not one of Ray as a companion. I really liked him. He was interesting, a pleasant and personable fellow. My problems with him came whenever I relied on him to make arrangements.

The men and women were celebrating in two separate areas. The women were grouped in a big circle picnicking, talking and generally feeling good to be seeing people outside of their usual compounds. The men were gathered in an area above which included two shacks. Upon entering, we saw two well-dressed western styled women, one of whom was truly beautiful. They were hanging out with the men, smoking cigarettes and generally appearing very lusty. Some of the men touched them lightly. Their presence seemed incongruous — here were two sophisticated, good looking women in this dirty shack with a bunch of crude tribesmen. One of the women noticed that I was "entranced" with her and she threw me a kiss and then signalled, I guess, that we should go off somewhere, a situation which would have been untenable since there would be no discretion. When we asked people about them nobody seemed to know where they came from or who brought them. I know they weren't friends of the bride's.

After about a half hour, Ray and I decided to split. Frankly, the situation was boring and yet a little weird. The tension inside the hut hung like an opaque cloud over the entire room. The odors of sex, desire and the flowing juices of excitement were too much for Ray to take. I was getting uncomfortable too. Our attendance put an edge on the whole situation.

We decided to walk back to the house and then I left for the hike back to the hotel

The next day we met at the bar as planned, in the morning. One of my new friends met us and we started the hour-long drive into the valley. As we turned the corner, Ray could not believe his eyes. There was the impressionist canvas I had described to him, but now in midday, the lines were etched sharper with more contrast from the overhead sun. Each family was working in its little plot, harvesting with a scythe, then laying the plants in the field to dry or bundling the plants to take them into the village to dry. In this village everyone seemed to be working, both men and women and even the kids.

Ray said that he had never seen a field or mountain as intensely cultivated as this. With our hosts' permission, we went into the fields for close examination. Ray was looking for the smelliest plants. Most of the plants had a very mild smell, more vegetative than grasslike. Once in a while he came across one that had a faint aroma of an Afghani or Indica. A few were sweet smelling. But most of them had very little odor.

I was examining the different cultivation techniques. Plants grown further apart had some branching as did the plants on the perimeter of the plots. Plants grown close together, similar to the way hemp is grown, have virtually no branching, and only one cola. Plants deprived of adequate amounts of moisture or nutrients were smaller and matured earlier than plants grown to full potential. While the rest of the plots were browning out, first turning a pale green, then yellow as they were harvested, one plot had plants still growing vigorously. They were still a deep green and the buds, though larger than any I had seen in the valley, were still immature, needing another two weeks before harvest.

The entire valley was irrigated using a series of open concrete troughs and ditches to supply each field with water. To get water into an individual plot, the farmer would open a gate, usually a piece of plywood with a few large stones to support it. There seemed to be more than adequate supplies of water.

Ray and I spent the better part of the afternoon investigating the fields, and then smoking hashish and learning how to make it.

To make just a little, our host took a porcelain bowl and tied a kerchief tightly around it using the four ends of the cloth. Next, he took about a pound of dried colas and rubbed them between his hands until they were ground into a coarse flour, sort of like wheat bran. Sticks, twigs, and seeds were separated from the leafy material. He did it by hand, but sometimes sieves are used. He placed about 2 ounces of the pure leaf on the tightened cloth screen and then he gently rubbed it across the cloth using both hands. After less than a minute, the material was removed and replaced with fresh flour. The used material was not discarded, but would be reused to make an inferior quality hash from the second rubbing. In five or six minutes he had rubbed the entire pound. The rubbing removed the glands which covered the plants. These THC glands settled in the bottom of the bowl. They made up a fine powder, with a consistency between fresh white and whole flour, but colored beige with maybe just a hint of a light lime green. The color was determined by the shade of the starting material. He took the loose flour and wrapped in cellophane (not plastic) and then in a piece of aluminum foil. He heated it over a candle and put it on the floor and stomped on it with the heel of his boot. He let the package cool for about ten minutes and then unwrapped a thin piece of hashish. This was the freshest hash that I had ever smoked.

We stayed overnight in the house overlooking the valley. The sun rising on the field was a beautiful sight.

Now my camera would not work. The battery had died overnight. My host said, "I have a camera just like it" and he pulled out a slightly different model from the same series which I used with my lenses. This was incredible. Even here in this small village, people have the use of state-of-the-art technology. We went down to the fields to spend the rest of the morning.

Our hosts were pretty incredible people. They spoke Arabic as their native language, but through intercourse with Europeans who travel through the area they also picked up French, which is Morocco's second language, German, English, and a little Italian and Spanish. Although they were living in a remote area, they had acquired through trade all sorts of modern consumer electronics and were interested in the world view.

Ray's friends were waiting for us when we got back to the hotel. We could see the relief showing on their faces. We explained that we had been treated most cordially, been given the freedom of the village and were not implored to buy anything.

I waited another two days but neither Ray's friends nor mine were able to come up with a commercial hashmaking set-up in operation. I was getting bored so I decided to head back to Casablanca. Ray said that he wanted to go with me as far as Fez. We made plans to leave the next day.

We hired a Mercedes to take us to a place where we could hire another taxi to Fez. There were no taxis available and we sat by the village taxi stand waiting for one to arrive. Across the square we spied a soup shop and for about a quarter we had a pretty refreshing snack. Meanwhile, the night was taking hold. Ray said that it would be difficult to find a hotel in the town. I doubted it because it seemed pretty large and had a big commercial area.

I don't like to travel country roads at night for several reasons. First, they are unsafe because of the construction, how they wind, and secondly, travelers are easier to prey upon. Finally a taxi arrived and Ray negotiated with the guy to drive us to Fez for 150 Durham, about five times the usual price. I was suspicious. I didn't like the smell of the thing — the guy was asking for too much and the situation was touchy. We got into the cab. Instead of taking the turn onto the road, the driver parked right outside the police station and went inside. Two officers came out to escort Ray and me into the courthouse.

The officers were not threatening and were even friendly. They had us open our suitcases and started searching for contraband.

Obviously the taxi driver figured that we were smugglers because we were willing to pay such an outrageous rate to get to Fez. His incentive to turn us in had both positive and negative potential consequences. Should his theory prove correct, he would reap a reward. However, should he give us a ride and the police find drugs on us during a roadcheck, he would be severely beaten.

The police could see that we had no kilos or even ounces of hash on us. They were about to close one of the suitcases when one officer decided to look in one of the plastic film cannisters. He opened it and out spilled some seeds. They all thought it was funny. He took the seeds on to the palm of his hand and gestured for me to eat them. I did. They laughed. One of the other officers took it just a little more seriously and found a few more seed cannisters. Then one of the officers said in broken English "You grow keif in America?" and they all laughed again. They pondered for a little while, first taking our names, passport number, addresses, etc. Then Ray said "America-Morocco good friends." The officer who had me eating out of the palm of his hand said in response, "President Reagan, King Hussein good friends." We all agreed, but then the officer saw my marijuana belt buckle and said "tsk, tsk."

Ray started up again, "Morocco food is very good." The officer who spoke little English finally understood and asked Ray, "You like it?" Ray said that he thought it was very good and the country had beautiful mountains, too. The officers deliberated for a few minutes more, then let us close our suitcases and escorted us back to the taxi for the ride to Fez. I was amazed. We had kept our cool and now we were shaking their hands as they wished us bon voyage. All but two of the cannisters were still in the suitcase. There was still a question — would these cops notify authorities to pick us up on the way out? This is not a healthy question to deliberate.

There were five of us in the taxi. The driver, Ray, myself, a soldier on leave, and another guy. They were frankly surprised to see us reemerge from the situation. The driver wasn't thrilled either. Obviously, we weren't guilty, so there was no reward. Even worse, we two who he had wronged by accusation were still going to ride with him for several hours to the city of Fez. The two other passengers seemed to be treating him with contempt. Not a word was spoken for the rest of the trip down the mountains. The driver could not enter Fez because he had no permit to pass the city checkpoint with his vehicle. We waited by the side of the road. The other people waiting were all Moroccans. And one by one drivers gave them rides. Finally, one driver stopped and was willing to give us a ride at three times the price charged Moroccans, but only if he could search our suitcases for contraband. Since he was looking for bricks or other forms of hash bulk, we agreed. We opened our bags, he felt no slabs,and we were off.

Fez was only about twenty minutes away, but near the gates to the city there was a roadblock. Seeing two Europeans in the car (us), the police pulled it over, and had us pull out our luggage. As we were doing this I noticed that all the Europeans were being pulled over. A middle-aged Frenchman with wife and two young kids were arguing with an officer, about fifteen feet away. We opened our cases, he shined his flashlight on the contents, then bent down, felt around inside, and motioned that we were free to go. Ten minutes later were were in Fez checking into our hotel.

The next day I went to the Moroccan airlines to get my reservations changed so that I could leave Morocco earlier. Unfortunately, their computer was down and they said that they would not be able to help me. Instead, I would have to change them in Casablanca. I got on the train and bid Ray a fond farewell.

The next day in Casablanca, the airline told me that there was only a slight chance of catching the next plane to leave, or even the one after that, but they could assure my passage in 10 days. I went back to the hotel and hoped for the best. Meanwhile my money was running low so I decided to use one of my credit cards. The bank would accept only Visa but not until checking with the States. They never got an answer.

The following day I went to the American Embassy. The people from States who run these outposts of America are especially chosen for their antisocial behavior and sadism. They pride themselves on using foreign authorities to ensnare hapless Americans and have no sensitivity to native cultures. I knew this from my trip to India. A friend of mine, who was studying there, invited me to the American Club, located inside the American Embassy compound in New Delhi. They have an American style dinner there and topping the menu are steaks and hamburger. India has primarily a Hindu culture and religion. The cow is a sacred symbol. Eating cow is repulsive to Indians the way eating dog or cat is to

Americans. Water buffalo, which tastes almost the same as cow, could be used on the menu with no insult to the Indians. As it is now, most Americans would be embarrassed to take an Indian to that dinner.

Anyway, when I went to the consulate, the consul handed me a sheet which described how the agency helped Americans to secure more money. The fastest way was to have the money wired to the State Department in Washington, with instructions to forward the credit to the consulate. Following regulations they assisted me in reaching my party in California who agreed to send money by the instructions I was given. If everything went right the money should arrive the next day, or at the worst, in two days.

When I checked back two days later, the money still had not arrived. I called my friend again, and she told me that she had sent the money to the Bank of Morocco instead of the consulate. Now time was critical. I might be able to leave in three days but I needed money to close out affairs.

Here again I was in a fix because I had not taken responsibility, but had allowed someone else to convince me that everything would be taken care of. Ray had assured me that he intended to cover all of my costs, so I had taken only $500 cash and credit cards. But MasterCard and Visa are not widely accepted by financial organizations in Morocco and I had had to pay for my room and was now waiting time in Morocco. These were expenses that Ray had told me not to anticipate. It was not his fault though, it was mine, because I had not taken the time to anticipate the possibilities for unexpected events.

The July 4th holiday was coming up which was a long weekend for the consulate, so that it could be of no help to me until after my hoped-for flight was scheduled to leave.

I called another friend and he sent the money to the State Department, but it did not arrive there on Friday, an hour before the consulate was to close. I was sitting on the couch there wondering what to do when a couple who were haggling with the agency came over to me and asked me if everything was OK. I was overcome. Here I was, going down, and out of nowhere Nourridene and Jennifer asked me if everything was OK. I explained that I needed some cash but had a tape recorder, cameras and other stuff I could sell and so on. They said, "Don't worry, come with us, to my cousin's house, and we can talk about it."

The house was about half-mile from the consulate in a nice neighborhood. During our walk over I explained my predicament and they agreed to buy my tape recorder and to take a check for about $40. This would give me all that I needed to take care of expenses and board the plane. We spent the afternoon together and they told me their story.

Jennifer had studied Arabic and Arab culture in school. She had met Nourridene in America, briefly. When she arrived in Morocco to continue her studies she and Nourridene met by chance.

They were very much in love, and wanted to live together in the States. Since Nourridene was a Moroccan citizen, he would not be able to leave, nor would he be granted resident alien status in the U.S. unless they were married. Under Moroccan laws, a woman is never independent. First, she is her father's ward and then her husband's. Since Jennifer was traveling alone, she was the consulate's ward. In order for the two of them to marry she needed the permission of the U.S. government, which was to come momentarily. Anyway, we spent the afternoon together, and they offered to put me up should I get bumped from my weekend flight.

We parted and I went back to my hotel to make final preparations for flying out the following day. I got to the airport 3 hours before flight time, but the scene was a madhouse. A couple at the counter was arguing with the reservations clerk. They were en route to America after teaching in Egypt for 2 years. They had hundreds of pounds of luggage in 6 footlocker-sized trunks, plus boxes, and had stopped over for what they had thought was a week. Now they were being told that their stay had been extended. There was no record of their reservation and the clerks had no explanation of how the ticket had been written. At that moment I knew that I was not going to be able to get the plane out. Instead, I sat on one of my bags (which I chose when purchasing for situations just like this; a place to sit when there were no other accomodations available.)

While I was sitting there, a sophisticated Arab-looking fellow came up and started to speak to me in French. I explained in the few French words at my disposal that I preferred English or could understand Spanish. He immediately continued the conversation in English and asked me if I would watch his bags. When he came back, he said that he, too, had been bumped from the flight. We decided to travel back to the city together and he told me a little about himself.

His name is Michael Vu, a French citizen living in Morocco. He is a watercolor and oil painter and lives in a small, remote town outside of the tourist beat. He spends his time painting scenes of the environment and the people he sees. He was on his way to Los Angeles for his first one-man show there.

While waiting for the bus we met another traveler. A nurse who had been working in Saudi Arabia. She had stopped over in Casablanca for a few weeks in Morocco, for some R&R. We took the bus back to the city and decided that the first priority was getting Michael's ticked adjusted. By now, I could home in on the Morocco Airlines office from any direction. I cannot say that the office manager was delighted to see my charming smile. He had already assured me my reservations on the next flight out, and coded my ticket for non-bumping. Michael spoke with him a few minutes, got his ticket adjusted, and then we went searching for something to eat. Michael ordered the three of us a delicious half-French, half-Moroccan meal.

Charlotte, the nurse, started to tell us stories of Saudi Arabia. She worked in a super modern hospital which catered to the tribespeople. Sometimes sheepherders would demand to be hospitalized with part of their herd. They did not want to be separated from their loved ones. Doctors had to go through weird procedures to operate on female patients. The Saudis buy gold by the handful. They take beautiful jewelry, put it on a scale, and flash the equivalent of $2000–$3000. They chase white women who literally are not safe because they are not respected. She caused a scene in a bank and again in a store when she would not let the men push ahead of her. She said she was not renewing her contract even though the pay was very good. But she was saving enough to continue her life which she felt had been placed on hold for the last two years.

Michael decided to go back to his village for the next few days and invited me. It was a long, torturous bus trip so I decided to stay in Casablanca. The nurse decided to go to one of the resort areas Michael suggested.

I decided to take Jennifer and Nourridene up on their offer. I handed the taxi driver the slip of paper on which Nourridene had written his address in Arabic. It was in a part of the city that few westerners ever get to see, often called the popular district. I guess they figured it was popular because so many people lived there. I got out of the cab, and when people saw me looking around for the correct house, they directed me to Nourridene's apartment. He lived with his parents and two sisters and Jennifer. Jennifer said that she was not surprised to see me, that she had expected me several hours ago. We hung out until Nourridene came and gave me a tour of the area. It was densely populated but the apartments were large, since there were usually 5 or 6 kids in the family. First we went to one of his hangouts and then to the cafe. The place had excellent cappucinos and fine French pastry. Life in the district was OK. I witnessed a wedding celebration, visited a photo studio, went to the cafes, and hung around getting stoned.

Nourridene was happy to cop hash for me. I had none since my travels down the mountains. This stuff was better than the farmers'.

That evening, Nourridene, who had dozens of cousins, met with two of them and several friends to play Moroccan music. The instruments included several drums, a guitar, another stringed instrument and voices. The music had a rhythm that flowed into my brain and let me drift into another state of consciousness. My task was keeping the hash pipe stuffed.

Over the weekend I went to the beach with the family. Nourridene explained that his parents were quite extraordinary. His mother was a Berber, a descendant of the mountain tribespeople whom I had recently visited. They are of Celtic stock, light-skinned with a lot of redheads. Nourridene's father met her and fell in love. Eventually their parents agreed. This was quite different from the ordinary pattern, where the parents arrange marriages with the consent of the children. Often the new couple have barely met.

Nourridene's father owned a thread factory, and had been partners with Moroccan Jews. When they left the country, his father had to redevelop the business.

The two daughters in the family were 17 and 21. One of them was still going to school and the other was working for National Cash Register training to be a computer programmer. Although she was working for this American conglomerate, they did not pay her — her training, they felt, was payment enough. Both of them had no socializing experiences with male friends and acted as though they were young teenagers. They were both tense, bored, and frustrated by the society.

Jennifer and Nourridene were still having trouble with the authorities. Nourridene had to go to another town twice to get papers signed. The first time the authorities would not process the documents because of a missing seal. Finally, after another two days the papers were signed. I was to leave at 2 p.m. the next day, giving me enough time to give the bride away and be a witness.

Jennifer and I went to the American Consulate to get the rest of her documents. The Consul had a look of total disgust when he saw the two of us walk in. We were probably his greatest hassles with Americans in months, and here we together. He handed Jennifer the papers, informed me that no money had arrived for me either at the consulate or the bank, and said sarcastically to Jennifer, "Good luck!"

Dragging my suitcase we went to the civic center. There, each judge, who was also a mullah or priest, had a little office, crammed to the brim with papers, documents, and files, in a crazy satire of bureaucracy. Nourridene had conferred with one judge several times who had directed him through the bureaucratic maze. But when we got to the office, the judge said that he couldn't handle the marriage for 10 days. Nourridene was flabbergasted. We went to another judge and he said that the documents would have to be checked for authenticity. A third judge said that he just couldn't do it. Nourridene and Jennifer weren't too upset by the refusals. They saw it as just another tangle to untie. Nourridene thought that his friend the judge wanted a bribe in addition to his regular fee. Nourridene, however, was adamant. They had come this far without succumbing to bribery and they weren't going to give in now.

My time was running out. I grabbed a cab and went to the airport. Michael and I met and had a couple of drinks with some of my last Moroccan money, and took I off for New York.

Postscript:

Michael Vu's show in Los Angeles was a success.

Jennifer and Nourridene did finally get married in Morocco and are now living in the Midwest.

Ray is working as a chauffeur in New England and living in a primitive shack without running water or electricity.

One of my two valley friends was arrested for rowdiness and is still in jail.

The Consul remains the mean, unpersonable fellow he always was.

Dr. Carlton Turner in his former office at the University of Mississippi.

Chapter Sixteen
Ed Rosenthal Interviews Carlton Turner

From pot farmer to dope czar! This sounds like the secret dream of a Humboldt County cannabis cultivator. In 1981 it was achieved by a good old boy from the deep South, when Ronald Reagan reached out and plucked Dr. Carlton Turner from the sultry bayou bottomland of Louisiana and installed him as the White House special adviser on drugs. For ten years, from the time he finished grad school, Carlton Turner occupied himself at the Ole Miss pot farm. There he raised marijuana for the use of credential-laden administrators of six-digit Federal grants award by the National Institute on Drug Abuse (NIDA). His main appearances, outside of University, Mississippi, had been made on behalf of the American Council on Marijuana and Other Psychoactive Drugs, Inc., a privately funded antigrass lobby on Capitol Hill, on which Dr. Turner has served as scientific adviser since 1980. But in 1981, when the Reagan people wanted a congenial personality to preside over drug abuse issues, Dr. Turner was abruptly enthroned in Washington. Yet his only area of expertise is the chemistry and botany of *Cannabis sativa L.* How could this have come to pass?

Well, consider James Watt, running the Department of the Interior after a lifetime of lobbying to open wilderness areas for exploitation by the industrial interests he represented. The Reagan people liked to appoint foxes to guard chicken coops, that's all. So Dr. Turner was the particular fox for the marijuana coop.

His main aim at the Ole Miss pot farm, as he candidly told me, was always to find things in marijuana that would "enhance the economy of the State of Mississippi through the pharmaceutical industry." This search mainly took the form of isolating, from the "crude drug *Cannabis*," the agent delta-9 tetrahydrocannabinol (THC), so that its molecular structure could be synthesized by commercial drug companies, which would modify it just enough so that it could be patentable for them as Nabilone (Eli Lilly), levantradol (Pfizer), and whatnot. This crude drug kills mild pain, reduces inflammation, quells nausea, promotes drowsiness, and has over 20 other clearly identifiable pharmacological effects. It was Turner's mission at Ole Miss to help find which part of the plant did what, so that its various active components could be counterfeited, and eventually merchandised, by the big drug companies.

The tough part was keeping the lid on cannabis itself, while glorifying the various synthetic preparations. Thus, Turner was never comfortable talking about "marijuana, the crude drug," as he calls it. In fact, it makes him exquisitely uncomfortable whenever he has to address the fact that his immaculate synthetics are always tainted by association with this crude herb. Here's Carlton Turner before a flock of pharmaceuticals magnates at a banquet meeting of the American Council on Marijuana, 1980: "As a pure substance, single in nature, made synthetically in the laboratory, delta-9 THC doesn't know the *Cannabis* plant nor the crude drug, marijuana, exist."

Unfortunately they do exist, as naturally occurring organic entities, and therefore this pure, single delta-9 THC is unpatentable. This makes the pharmaceutical industry very nervous. Some people suspect that the industry might even oppose a relaxation of legal restraints on marijuana, just to cut down on competition with their glorious future THC homologues.

As for the evidence Dr. Turner cites to support his gloomy views on the crude herb itself, well, consider that he also cites *The Decline and Fall of the Roman Empire* (presumably to conjure up a vision of how jazz singers and their white-liberal groupies are eroding the general cultural fabric with this hallucinogen). Pharmacology is not Turner's long suit. Before he cited them in this 1978 interview, the health brain-damage reports had already been amply discredited for biased methodology. But NIDA, which funded his work at Ole Miss, had published a Berkeley study showing that an ounce of grass yields precisely 1.5 times as many potential carcinogens as an ounce of tobacco; that is, when you smoke a joint the size of a Lucky, you're taking in a Lucky-and-a-half's worth of potential carcinogens.

At the time this interview was conducted, Dr. Turner was still running the Federal pot farm. I went down to Ole Miss to lock horns with the good doctor about Federal drug policy. By the time we'd finished, I was really concerned that the government's house expert was so completely naive about drugs. With all the pot Turner had grown, he claimed he'd never gotten high. Never had a 'lude or dropped acid. Nothing. I think, based on personal experience, that I'm probably better qualified than Turner is to run NIDA and the FDA.

Preparing samples at the University of Mississippi laboratory.

Ed: What is the relationship between you, the government, and the university?

Turner: I'm an employee of the Research Institute of Pharmaceutical Sciences [RIPS], which is located in the School of Pharmacy at the University of Mississippi. The Research Institute was created in 1964 by an enabling act of the stage legislature. Our job is to enhance the economy of the State of Mississippi through the pharmaceutical industry. It is the only institute that I know of anywhere in the world that is funded as a line item from the state legislature, is housed in an academic department, and is really dovetailed with academia. Each member of the university staff must do research, since RIPS has a mandate to enhance the state's economy through research.

In my own private research, I have been involved in *Cannabis* since 1970. I am also involved in ethnic cosmetics as a pharmacognosist, which is a person interested in drugs of natural origin. I also have an academic title, which I don't have reason to use, and I'm the associate director of RIPS, which means I'm responsible for funding and executing in-house research programs. This defines what is happening in Mississippi.

My relationship with the government is that I am strictly a contractor and a grant holder from NIDA (National Institute on Drug Abuse). I have a protocol which I must execute, and I must run this in the most economically feasible way to save tax dollars.

Ed: *What is the purpose of the current grant?*

Turner: The current grant is the separation of nitrogenous compounds from the *Cannabis* plant. It is funded by NIDA. The grant was originally for twenty-one or twenty-two thousand dollars. We've found several nitrogenous compounds: hordenine, which is a beta-arylethyl amine. It's not unheard of in plants but we didn't expect to find it in *Cannabis*. Then we found two compounds of a totally different structure. They're spermidine-type alkaloids, and this is the first time they've been found to exist in higher plants. One of them is called cannabisativine and the other, hydrocannabisativine. These are interesting in the chemotaxonomy of the *Cannabis* plant.

Since I have a contract from NIDA, if I'm going to talk about something they've sponsored, they should know who I'm talking to, and I have to be responsible for everything I say. Not that they're going to tell me what I can say. I've never had anyone in the Federal government say, "You can't publish that," or "You can't say this." I've never had anyone at the school or RIPS say, "You can't do this, you can't do that." But I've always tried to be honest and considerate of other people's feelings, and tried to be scientific, instead of trying to be a promoter or a crusader.

Ed: *How did you get into working in this area?*

Turner: I got a degree in organic chemistry, as a synthetic organic chemist working on plant growth regulators, in 1970. In 1970 organic chemists were a dime a dozen. I took the only available job that I was qualified for, which was a postdoctoral research associate position in the Department of Pharmacology in the School of Pharmacy at the University of Mississippi. I came here with the idea of spending one year learning something about marijuana and then going to law school.

In 1971 I was asked to assume responsibility for the project; at that time I felt I was the only one here who could, so I accepted, and it's been a rat race ever since.

Ed: Have your feelings about marijuana changed since you started working with this program?

Turner: I think my feelings about the crude drug marijuana have been broadened tremendously. In 1970 people said that everything there was to know about marijuana was known. And how wrong they were! But as for my being scientifically concerned, I haven't changed.

Ed: What is the purpose of the program you're involved in?

Turner: The purpose is to provide NIDA with a standard grade of marijuana for research. When we say a standard grade of marijuana, we mean one whose content we know within analytical limits. There are a total of 61 cannabinoids known, so there are many cannabinoids we know very little about as far as analytical methods are concerned. The batch we prepare today for a research purpose may not be the same three years from now.

We give the best-defined materials available to NIDA and to the research community. This material is also used by the U.N. narcotics laboratory, so it goes all over the world. We are primarily here for this part of our program. To execute and accomplish this, you must have a growing facility, some good analytical support facilities, isolation-separation facilities, and the ability to export and import to get variants from different geographical locations.

Ed: In any given year do you provide more than one standard grade?

Turner: We have a Mexican variant which is our standard drug type. Mexican variant from location A is not the same as Mexican variant from location B, but the one we're using is the one that was selected in 1968 as the drug type. We've been extremely satisfied with it. We've grown the Mexican since 1968 and we haven't seen the deterioration of potency that people talk about. The drug type is the one that all the INDs (investigative new drug applications) are operating under. When you talk about Mexican, there's only one variant that has an IND.

Ed: How does this variant rate in THC content?

Turner: Delta-9 THC content is something that you can't put your finger on. You can go out and take a sample and analyze it and say, "This is Mexican; it has 2.1 percent THC." That tells you the analysis of one cannabinoid out of a total of 61, out of a total of roughly three hundred sixty-odd chemicals in the plant. We can produce a good drug, marijuana, from this Mexican variant. It is as good as you will get without going through a great deal of sophisticated agricultural procedures.

Ed: People often say that different varieties of Cannabis give different highs: speedy, work-oriented, laid-back. Would you say that the interaction of these different cannabinoids relates in some way to this?

Turner: You've got to take into consideration the interaction of the cannabinoids. We know that cannabidiol (CBD) antagonizes and cannabinol potentiates some of the effects of delta-9. We don't know what kind of effect cannabichromene has on delta-9, but all potent drug types contain it and rarely, if ever, do they contain any CBD. These are just four cannabinoids we're talking about. The research that has been done is primarily on delta-9 or delta-8 or some of the synthetic cannabinoids, so you've got to go back and look at the plant material. This crude drug marijuana is not a plant; it's a crude drug taken from the *Cannabis* plant.

If we take this crude drug and roll it into a joint, the drug quality — or the amount of the cannabinoids coming through the smokestream — will depend on the compactness, the porosity of the paper, the humidity of the material, the particle size, and the puff volume. These are the five main variables. So, when you get a different joint, you get a different ratio of these cannabinoids.

I would expect the different marijuanas to give different highs. I could go out to a single *Cannabis* plant, select a sample at eight in the morning, and process it into marijuana; if I went out again at ten to the same plant, I'd expect to get another marijuana. And I'd expect those two to give you different-grade highs.

You see, the cannabinoids are a unique class of compounds in nature, and they're very hard to work with. I think we're probably the only people who have done a lot of extractions to see what the conditions are in which you get the most cannabinoids out of the plant.

Ed: When you test, what part of the plant do you use?

Turner: We use the leaf part.

Ed: Do you use the bud? Do you grow sinsemilla?

Turner: No. When you run it through a cigarette machine, the tiny-sized particle is going to be kicked right out. So you've got to get a leaf that's large enough to go through a cigarette machine, that's large enough to be sliced so you can make a good-sized particle out of it with the bracts still in there.

Ed: Then if your material tests at, let's say arbitrarily, 2 percent THC, then actually the flowering buds might test at 3, 4, or 5 percent THC.

Turner: Some cigarettes analyzed at up to 2.68, and that's after it's been processed into a cigarette.

Ed: When do you harvest?

Turner: We harvest the plant at the point when it has the cannabinoids we desire for our research program, whether it's twelve weeks old or twenty weeks old. We don't wait until it comes into flower, because when you're growing in a large garden area, you can't cut all the males out. When you've got over five acres, there are going to be some males. That little flowering top is not going to do a darned thing as far as making a cigarette is concerned.

Ed: Can high-quality marijuana be grown anywhere in the United States?

Turner: Sure. The South African material has been grown in South Africa, Mississippi, and Norway — above the Arctic Circle — and the data are so close that if I didn't know the studies had been done independent of each other, I'd say someone was gilding the lily.

Ed: Do you use any special fertilizers?

Turner: We have a soil sample taken and find out what area of our garden grows best, and then we try to duplicate that.

Ed: Do you do any pruning?

Turner: No.

Ed: Have you ever tried to simulate either climatic or soil conditions from exotic areas?

Turner: No. That is totally outside the realm of what I'm interested in, and also outside what the [NIDA] program could afford.

Ed: Do you think altitude has anything to do with THC content?

Turner: We are in the process of publishing a paper on altitude. Ideally you should take the same type of seed and plant it in different geographical locations, then analyze them over a long period of time and look at the total profile. But what the botanist did was to make collections at a certain time of year, with the idea that these samples had been unmolested by man for a long time, so that this should give us some idea of what effects the altitude variation would give us over a period of time.

Ed: What time would you harvest?

Turner: Very early in the morning. It follows a cyclic pattern. You'd have to do an analysis over a period of weeks to find out exactly.

Ed: Do you feel that THC generates and regenerates over a 24-hour cycle?

Turner: I don't know. I don't think anyone knows. There is a fluctuation with time. Just as our biorhythms change, these cannabinoids change with time. I don't know where they go, but this indicates that the plant is using them in some sort of metabolic way. I don't really know how to explain it.

Ed: Over a 24-hour period, you'll get different analyses of a particular leaf, and [the cannabinoids] will go up during the dark hours and down during the light hours?

Turner: That's an indication, but it's not an absolute fact. You may run four or five days when the fluctuation will be significant, but the baseline data will be the same; then the next week the baseline data may go up and there may not be as much fluctuation. You can't say absolutely, "During the dark hours this is going to happen," or "During the day hours it's going to happen." It depends a lot on the variants: on the chemical makeup of the plant regarding the cannabinoids, and on what the plant needs, if we assume that the cannabinoids are being metabolized by the plant. I can't say categorically that they are, and I can't say they aren't.

Ed: What do you think the purposes of the cannabinoids are to the plant?

Turner: I don't know.

Ed: Is anybody doing research on that? Or are there any theories on it?

Turner: There are many theories that its function is as a protective coating. According to some people, it is also some protection from predators, but if you mean knowing with a great deal of fact to back you up, no one really knows.

Ed: Would a hemp-type Cannabis plant ever be resiny even though it contained mostly CBD?

Turner: Resin is by definition the water-insoluble components of the plant. The most resinous plants I have seen have been grown from the Czechoslovakian and Lebanese seed. They exude resin. However, the THC content is extremely low. Hash coming from Morocco and the Czech material have a lot more CBD than they do THC. Yet you will find more resin in these two plants at our facility than we've seen in any other plant. The Mexican material is a very potent drug type, but you don't see resin on the buds. You have to rub them in your hands real tight and crush them to get the resin on your fingers.

Ed: I saw some Afghani this year that had an almost skunklike odor, and it was very resinous. You mentioned Lebanese and Moroccan, and I mentioned Afghani. All of those are plants from around the thirtieth latitude.

Turner: The Afghan, Moroccan, Lebanese, Pakistani, many of the Indians, and the Nepalese usually have more CBD than delta-9.

Ed: I think that's why all of those plants traditionally have been concentrated into hashish.

Turner: They would make very bad marijuana.

Ed: Although Afghani I have tried has been potent as well as tasty.

Turner: This is an anomaly.

Ed: How does THC get one high?

Turner: I don't know.

Ed: Do you have any ideas along those lines?

Turner: We know that the 11-hydroxyl metabolite is an active psychotropic-type compound. We also know that the hydroxylated compounds on the side chain without the hydroxyl in the 11 position, using the delta-9 nomenclature, also get you high. But what chemical mechanism it triggers in the brain to cause that, we don't know. And our knowledge of brain chemistry is in the embryonic stage.

Ed: Do you know what constituent of marijuana causes the munchies?

Turner: No. I've heard the munchies mentioned, but not having firsthand experience, and not really being concerned with the munchies, that's all I know about it.

Ed: There definitely is something in marijuana that causes smokers, especially inexperienced ones, to get a craving for food.

Turner: If that's the case, we ought to see a lot of fat marijuana smokers, because they ought to eat a lot. I don't see a lot of fat marijuana smokers around.

But if you take into consideration that you're dealing with an awful lot of compounds in the *Cannabis* plant that have a strong affinity for brain cells and for the fat cells and the various proteins in the body, then these compounds get from the bloodstream into the brain, you would expect anything to happen according to what side of the brain they come into, how they are stored in the brain, and how they are handled in the brain.

Ed: What do you think the future of marijuana will be in America?

Turner: I'll be happy to give you a scientific opinion based strictly on the facts as I know them. If you look at the literature related to marijuana today, you don't see much cause for optimism. That doesn't mean the illicit market is going to go out of business. But let's forget about the illicit marketeers and look at this crude drug, marijuana, and put blinders on, and just say we're going to go down the middle of the road and see what we know about this crude drug.

First of all, there are over six thousand papers in the literature. Now of the six thousand papers, most do not deal with marijuana. They deal with synthetic cannabinoids. However, certain individuals, organizations, advertising agencies, et cetera, have tried to extrapolate from the data and say that the cannabinoids are the same as marijuana. And there's a lot of misinformation about marijuana in these papers. From these six thousand papers, I could support any conceivable idea you might come up with of what marijuana will do or what cannabinoids will do. Let's now forget about the cannabinoids and run back to the crude drug, marijuana.

The second thing is that marijuana has to meet certain guidelines to get on the market. You have to go through an IND and then a NDA [new drug application]. Only one variant of marijuana, that is, the Mexican variant, is even at the IND stage.

Another problem that I see, or another possibility: What about the Delaney Amendment? Nobody has bothered to investigate the Delaney Amendment. Look at the cyclamates. In the late '60s, one article says that cyclamates cause bladder cancer in animals. Three hundred papers since then have not been able to duplicate that, and yet cyclamates are still not back on the market. We know that there are more cancer-causing agents in the smoke of one marijuana cigarette than in that of one tobacco cigarette. The smoke from one marijuana cigarette, when painted on laboratory animals, will cause cancer, so there's a statutory bar against *Cannabis* according to the Delaney Amendment.

The next thing is that you must have shelf-life stability on any drug before it goes to market. But the cannabinoids change over a period of time. And as these cannabinoids change, the quality of the drug changes. Now I'm not saying you couldn't set up a "plus-or-minus" criterion, but this is an inherent problem which must be solved before you can ever bring anything onto the market.

The future of marijuana as a crude drug I see as very, very bleak. I'm not saying that some of the compounds of the *Cannabis* plant, their homologues or analogues, will not be used by society. In its medical applications to disease states, I wouldn't say that at all.

Ed: The thing is, even with all the laws such as the Delaney Amendment, if Congress decides that it does not want the loss of Cannabis, it can just pass a law saying Cannabis can be grown for home cultivation or for commercial use, or whatever; and since Congress makes the laws, it has the power to change them.

Turner: I would not disagree with that.

Ed: Do you think it will be decriminalized on a state-to-state basis

Turner: I think there's de facto decriminalization in most states. I have quarreled with the word decriminalization; I think it's a bad choice of words because, to the average person, it means that you remove the criminal penalties. But you're not actually removing the criminal penalties. Most of the state laws I'm familiar with have reduced the penalty on the low end and raised the penalty for the smuggler or the big-time operator. I personally feel that reducing the penalty for the kid with one joint has not been a bad idea, and I was for it in Mississippi. But I was also for sending the guy who deals in hundreds of pounds to jail.

Ed: What about the home gardener cultivating for his or her own personal use?

Turner: The home gardener is an individual within himself or herself. How they handle it is up to each state; I'm not trying to make policies or make decisions. I'm just saying that, knowing what I know about that crude drug, I would hate to see it ever come to pass that we had home growing of *Cannabis* to produce the crude drug, marijuana. I'm afraid they'll go from marijuana to liquid hash, and a combination of more things. As you apply physical, chemical, or heat methods to process the *Cannabis* plant, you alter the chemical constituents, so the data on marijuana are not the data on delta-9, which are not the data on hashish. So I have a terrible fear, as a scientist, as to what would happen there.

Ed: In California the buds may go for a hundred dollars an ounce and the leaves for a hundred a pound. Those leaves may contain one-third to one-half the THC grown on the plant. It's only a matter of time before people start using them either as a ghee, or in cookies, or something like that.

Turner: When you take it orally you've got a different drug than when you smoke it; you have metabolism occurring in two different places, the lung and the liver. The metabolites in the lung are much more potent psychomimetic agents than the metabolites in the liver. This is one of the reasons people can get a much higher high by smoking a small amount than by eating a much larger amount, and these affect the body differently.

I'm fearful of the increasing potency, of the concentration of the cannabinoids in the tissues of the body. These things bother me as a scientist. But each individual has to make up his own mind what he wants to do. I don't believe the government should say, "Here it is, available to everybody, use it as [you] want to." But I don't really know what the proper position is right now. I know we don't have enough data to say that marijuana is an innocuous drug.

Ed: But we have to look at it from a societal level, too.

Turner: You have to consider the total scientific spectrum. In science you can't cut one layer out. You have to look at it in context: what it's doing to the human organism, what it's doing to society. My point is very basic. It is not an innocuous drug.

Look at tobacco. We know if we smoke × amount of tobacco cigarettes a day, our chances of getting lung cancer are × percent greater than those of the guy who never touches a cigarette. But I'll challenge you or anyone else to find me any sociological data, or any other kind of data, prior to World War II, that would link tobacco smoke with bronchial carcinoma. It did not exist. And now look at the people dying of lung cancer.

We know that *Cannabis* smoke contains as many carcinogenic compounds as a cigarette — more, in fact. We know that in our society people smoke several joints a day. We also know that as they grow for their own use, they're going to get more potent material, so there are some intrinsic problems. I do not want to say that sociological studies are not significant. But when you do sociological studies, you've got to do studies on the basis of how the people in our community use it, not how they do it in Jamaica or how they do it somewhere else.

Ed: What are the long-term effects of occasional and heavy marijuana use?

Turner: I don't think anyone knows in the society in which we're operating today.

Ed: What do you think of Reese Jones's experiments, where he's giving people tremendous doses of THC which don't really correspond to what's happening?

Turner: Can you say that?

Ed: Yes. I have experience with the underground culture, and he's talking about more than the heaviest smoker I've ever seen. Even when I've known people dealing in hash oil, they didn't use as much as he's giving to his people.

Turner: You don't know what's in hash oil until you analyze it. I've seen hash oil range from very small amounts of THC right up to 40 percent THC.

The other thing is, a lot of scientists have been criticized for the dosage they're giving. But there's a tremendous problem here. Smoking is the worst possible way to get a standardized dosage of any drug into the organism.

One researcher will tell his people, "Smoke this, you'll get a pleasant high." [He will] never quantitate the blood, never know how much is getting in, because until recently you couldn't do that. Another researcher will say, "I want you to smoke this in toto, because that's the only way I'll know what you're getting." Well, a two percent cigarette, one gram, will contain 20 milligrams. When both of these researchers publish their data (and you can get anything on marijuana published), it's quoted as law, and it's very difficult to change people's opinions once it's in print. A guy who says, "Smoke it, you'll get a pleasant high," is not going to find the same change in respiration rate, blood pressure, or pulse rate, if there is a change, as the person who makes them smoke all of it. The lay, and even the scientific, community, then says one of these guys is wrong. In reality both are correct according to their methodologies, but you have to find out which methodology is correct.

Until I see the data, until I see how it happens... I've seen a lot of people getting tremendous criticism of their dosage range; when I looked at the data, they were all using very small amounts.

Ed: What do you feel are the dangers of marijuana as compared with alcohol?

Turner: There are very different profiles when you look at alcohol and *Cannabis*. The body can handle alcohol quite rapidly. About one ounce per hour for the average person. And in a few hours, it's totally removed from the system. But the cannabinoids have a long staying power. For example, if you give a naïve subject one joint, after a period of fifty-six hours there is going to be at least half of the cannabinoids still in the system, and after eight days you can still find the cannabinoids.

The cannabinoids are totally insoluble in water, but they are infinitely soluble in the lipid proteins of the body. Which means they are stored in every major organ, including the brain. This means that after a long period of time there's going to be a residual amount of delta-9 and other cannabinoids.

If you smoke only one joint, and you don't smoke any more for a while, it gives your body an opportunity to sort of purge the system. But if you keep loading that system up, with three or four joints a day, one has to be concerned, knowing that the cannabinoids are stored in the brain and other places, over the long-term effects — not over the subtle differences of ninety days, that's ridiculous — but it is done every day. So my concern is basically with the long haul.

Ed: Is somebody who has smoked for twenty years going to have so much in their system that they're never going to get rid of it?

Turner: No one really knows. We're participating in a long-term study. I have a deep-seated fear about long-term use.

Ed: Does a nursing mother transfer the cannabinoids through her milk?

Turner: There's a paper that appeared in the *Journal of Toxicology* that shows there are a lot of problems. Milk has a lot of lipid-protein-type material and a lot of fat, and if the cannabinoids were to be stored, this would be one place you'd find them. If a young lady is smoking a lot of grass and she is nursing a baby, it's probably going to have cannabinoids in its system.

People say that marijuana causes birth defects. There has been no really good documentation of birth defects from using marijuana, but there have been documented embryocidal effects, which means that the embryo was reabsorbed. This indicates that the cannabinoids do interfere with the reproductive systems of the body. It is now looking very much as if it is more acute in the male than in the female. You see some testicular degeneration with CBD. CBD is one of the most abundant cannabinoids, particularly in hashish and in some forms of marijuana. So there is more than an average chance of problems over the long haul.

Ed: Do experienced marijuana smokers metabolize Cannabis in a different way than inexperienced smokers?

Turner: They have a lot of enzymes in the system that can handle it. I don't think anyone has isolated the enzymes that are responsible.

Ed: Have long-term changes been noted in the brain synapses of marijuana users?

Turner: Drs. Dick Gary and Bob Heath in New Orleans did some work on the monkey brain, and in every animal that had *Cannabis* or delta-9, they saw some problems in the synapses and in the brain. That is pretty hard evidence, and if this were a drug on the market, it would be pulled off immediately. There are also some changes in the electrocardiogram with chronic smoke.

Ed: Do you think that marijuana changes motivation?

Turner: Some people say that the amotivational syndrome is only a syndrome with those people doing the research. But if you talk with the people who work with *Cannabis*, marijuana, the cannabinoids, they will tell you that everything is dose-dependent, as with any drug. I think it has a lot to do with the biochemistry and maturity of the person involved and a lot of other things.

Ed: Do you think that the government can enforce the marijuana laws?

Turner: Enforcement of the laws is something that society wants one day and does not want the next day. It will be extremely difficult to enforce the laws of this country on the use of *Cannabis*. On the other hand, if the penalties were so severe that the use would not be worth the consequences if you were caught, you would reduce it. But as an objective individual, and knowing that you can grow

Cannabis anywhere, I think it would be impossible for the government to absolutely eradicate the use of *Cannabis* in this society. I don't think it can be done.

Ed: *If the penalties become so severe, considering that we have a representative government of some sort, I think that kind of law would alienate society as a whole from the government.*

Turner: An excellent example of that is Germany before World War II. Every power that Hitler had was given him by the legislative body. And everybody says that Hitler was a dictator.

Ed: *I think our experience is different from the German experience.*

Turner: Well, regardless of the political implications, if it were the death penalty, whether you or I agreed with it, I think both you and I agree that there's no way some of the people we know who use it would touch it with a ten-foot pole.

Ed: *I think that marijuana is one of America's secret weapons in our conflict with the Soviet Union. This could be one of the main things changing Soviet society, changing the Soviet government.*

Turner: Well, if it could change the Soviet government, it's changing our society too.

Ed: *It certainly is. How do you think it's changing our society?*

Turner: The value system of any society is based upon the learning pattern. What you're saying is that we're changing the learning pattern. We're basing our values somewhere else. I think that's where the sociologists have got to come out of the closet and get on with the job of finding out what's happening to our society.

Just as our society in the South has changed, I think any society's going to change, and change for change's sake sometimes happens. We hope it doesn't happen. We hope that we have a better society due to change. But if we study history, and we look at what's happening to our society, we ought to have some second thoughts. If you study Gibbon's *History of the World* [*sic*], it scares you if you look at what's happening to our society today.

Ed: *If individual states passed laws decriminalizing or legalizing marijuana, or its cultivation, do you think the DEA would stand still?*

Turner: I don't know. You'd have to ask someone in the DEA. But I don't see how the government could stand by and watch an international treaty, the FDA guidelines, and the laws of this country being totally neglected. It would be a precedent-setting thing that would open the door for any drug to go on the market without proper testing, because only one variant of *Cannabis* is in the IND.

Suppose the Federal government were to say, "We're going to make *Cannabis* available to everybody." Then suppose ten or fifteen years down the road we had a tremendous increase in neurological problems with young people and they traced that back to *Cannabis* in the brain. The same people who are pushing for these drugs to be on the market today would then be in their fifties or sixties, and they would be raising hell with the government because their daughters or their grandsons would have neurological problems and it would be the government's fault.

Ed: *Do you think that any of the government's programs are effectively informing people about marijuana or keeping people from using it?*

Turner: It's a difficult task, because preconceived ideas abound in the area of marijuana. Because if you're using it, whether it does you any harm or not, if it's a subtle amount that you can't observe daily, you're not going to see it, and you're going to say, "Nothing's wrong with this drug, and don't try to educate me about it, because I know more than you." I've talked to kids sometimes, not with scare tactics, but just talked to them, and I've had kids say, "Have you ever tried it?" I have no desire or need to try it. "Well, then don't talk to me about marijuana." The classical comeback is, "How many male obstetricians have you seen who have had a baby?"

As an organic chemist and pharmacologist, I have learned to have a great deal of respect for chemicals and for what they can do to the body, and I have never had any reason nor any desire to smoke a joint. I've always wanted to keep my mind clear. I enjoy nature, people, working and doing things with my hands, and when you get into an intoxicated level, whether with alcohol, *Cannabis*, or any other drug, when you are no longer in control, then things happen to you that later on you may wish had not happened to you.

Ed: Do you think that we're going to find in four, five, or ten years that preadolescents and adolescents who used marijuana have had deleterious effects from its use during the formative years?

Turner: If you take the biological data on marijuana now, you have got to be concerned about that.

Ed: What are the long-term effects of use of marijuana by preadolescents and adolescents?

Turner: I can't say what the long-term effects will be. We can only look at what the scientific data have indicated, and extrapolate. There is going to be a change. Whether that change is going to show up in the second or third generation, you can't say, but there will be a change.

Ed: How do you think that the government's attitude toward Cannabis has changed over the past three or four years?

Turner: I think as the trends go to much more potent material, you're going to find a hardening of the attitude on the Federal level, and some of the manipulation of the news media by the pro-marijuana people has turned the other people totally against them. The overzealous attitude of the pro-drug people backfired, and I think we're going to see a hardening at the Federal level.

Ed: What do you think is going to happen in Colombia?

Turner: Colombia has for many years been making more money on the export of *Cannabis* products than it has on coffee. And it is going to be extremely difficult to convince the governments of developing countries to do away with Cannabis. If our government tried to help the Colombian government, I don't know how people would react.

Ed: I've heard two things: they're going to legalize or start spraying. Two conflicting opinions, both from so-called informed sources. I've also heard that Jamaica was planning to start legalization.

Turner: I don't believe that Jamaica will legalize it. I don't believe there is any politician in the world today who could stand the heat from the other government agencies in the world if they did. And I don't believe the countries of the world would continue putting money into certain funds that are controlled to study drugs if they planned to legalize them.

Ed: What do you feel the cost of marijuana is to society, in terms of people who use it, and in terms of law enforcement?

Turner: I don't have any idea how many people smoke grass in this country today. I've seen estimates from nine million to twenty-five million, but I don't know whether these figures are valid statistically.

I think that some of the costs that I've seen have been grossly inflated. There is a baseline cost of police protection, regardless of whether they're chasing crooks, sitting on their butts, fighting fires, or whatever. That's a basic cost.

Ed: How do you think that Cannabis will be used pharmacologically?

Turner: There are possibilities for certain individual cannabinoids. There are some drawbacks. It affects the central nervous system. Secondly, you build up a tolerance to them.

Some products that may come to the marketplace will not have a name even remotely associated with marijuana or *Cannabis*, but the idea for the synthesis of these products will have originated with NIDA's total marijuana program. One that comes to mind now is Nabilone, which Lilly has been promoting, but that's not to say there aren't others around. But it's hard for me to conceive of delta-9, with the side effects that it has, ever being on the market. I believe there will be a product on the market that has structural similarities.

Ed: Is there anything else that you'd like to say?

Turner: I hope that you come up with something legitimate within itself, and that we give the people an opportunity to see both sides. I keep trying to reiterate: I have tried not to be anti or pro, but to look at the scientific facts. And I can back those facts up. And I would like for people to be aware of the tremendous volume of literature, and not to be caught defending their position on the basis of a single paper.